Identity Reclaimed

ECHOES OF AN ADOPTEE

JULIE WETHERBY

ENTITY
PUBLISHING
UK

Identity Reclaimed: Echoes of an Adoptee

Cover Design by Mamook Graphics Ltd.

Published by Entity Publishing UK

Author e-mail: jw.identityreclaimed@gmail.com

ISBN: 978-1-5272-0787-5

Author's Note

This is a true story. Everything that takes place in it actually happened. However, owing to the sensitive nature of the subject matter and in the interests of preserving anonymity, names have been changed. A few characters are amalgams, and there are also several alterations of gender with regard to more minor members of the cast. Apart from a few named places, some locations have been moved while others are non-specific. Dates have also been changed. Certain situations have therefore been tweaked in order to accommodate these liberties so that they do not disturb the narrative flow.

Dedicated to those affected by adoption:

Birth parents who cannot rewrite history
Adoptive parents who strive to make the best of things
Adoptees who once had no voice

CONTENTS

Introduction

This story began in my mind at the initial unfolding of the search into my past. Even in those first few days, when the mysteries of early life started to emerge, I knew I would write it, and since the question of identity was uppermost, realisation dawned. I had found the theme, it was the heart of the matter.

Additionally, I wanted to address something: the misconceptions commonly held by well-intentioned people that surround the subject of adoption. By extension, I grieve at the lack of understanding my adoptive parents had when they took me on, all those years ago. I wish so much that someone had been there to counsel them, help them understand the temper tantrums, the awkward questions, the times of withdrawal and unfathomable behaviours arising amidst what was, for the most part, a happy, loving childhood.

This led me to conduct some research, since the residue of this child remains, surfacing in scary fashion during my roller-coaster experiences when searching into my past, and connecting with its present day fallout. In particular I was led to the writings of Nancy Verrier. Her book 'The Primal Wound' has become an adoption bible in recent years. In it she explores the trauma caused by separation from the biological mother at an early age, no matter what the circumstances.

I also turned to an online article which first appeared in the 1996 spring edition of the 'Pre- & Perinatal Psychology Journal' entitled 'The Vulnerable Prenate', written by William Emerson PhD. Here he expounds the theory that pre-birth traumas are re-lived after birth. The findings are not, of course, the exclusive preserve of the adoptee, but they do examine what he considers to be the harmful effects of 'abortion ideation', when parental consideration of the act of abortion is felt as life-threatening to the unborn child. Dr. Emerson also refers to 'a broad range of experiences that are common to adoption'.

It is my sincere desire that my own personal story will help those who have not been adopted to understand those of us who are, a little better. And it is also my sincere desire that adoptees can, perhaps, understand themselves a little better too.

Julie Wetherby

Remember who you were before
they told you who to be.

Dulce Ruby

1

The Bombshell

I was ten – perhaps eleven – when the row with Mum broke out. The unleashing of anger born of frustration, deeper than a passing surface dispute, it came from a place far distant.

'Who am I?' my tortured words at last rang out from the apple orchard beside our house.

'You're our child of course.'

'But who am I really?' I insisted.

Mum was at a loss, she didn't seem to know the answer. I sulked, yet knew I'd achieved what I'd wanted: inflicted hurt, made her – made both my parents – suffer. And it wasn't going to go away, my need to know.

Despite this, I'd had what would be classed as a happy upbringing. We shared things as a family and I never heard Mum and Dad argue; I was quite amazed to learn that other children's parents did so. By the time they got married just after the second world war, they'd reached their late thirties. From years of hardship and suffering, something had been salvaged: love, and gratitude. And they were thankful to have salvaged something else, the chance to raise a child from babyhood as their own. An injustice put right, so it seemed.

My parents were therefore much older than those of my school friends, by at least ten years, a matter about which I was acutely embarrassed when I entered my teens in the swinging sixties. And I didn't look like them either, something I became more and more aware of as I grew older. My school friends commented on it, just as they commented on the fact that my parents looked older than theirs. Thus I was propelled from childhood into years of being – at times – an angry, thwarted, and bullied teenager, who gave her parents more hell than they deserved.

School. That seedbed of doubt. The place where I painted a picture of Mum in an art class when I was still quite young. Jet-black permed hair, rolled up at the base and pinned into place at the neck, skin a shade of pale pink which I achieved in my delight at mixing red poster paint with white, assigning, by similar procedure, a beautiful pale shade of green to her eyes. She was a good looking woman, my mum, and I handed in my completed painting to Mrs. Perkins – who taught us art – with pride. One day she brought it into the classroom to show Miss Jones, our new class teacher. Sitting in the front row of desks, I watched the two of them closely as they examined the painting. Both of them seemed to like it, there was even talk of putting it in a school art exhibition.

'But *is* this her mother?' Mrs. Perkins questioned,

with undisguised doubt. 'It was the topic I gave to the class – to paint a picture of their mother.'

'I suppose it is,' Miss Jones murmured doubtfully, 'I haven't met her yet.'

It was true, she hadn't, since I travelled on the school bus and parent evenings didn't yet exist in those days.

Noticing my proximity, Mrs. Perkins lowered her voice.

'It's just that I don't like disobedience – and lying.'

'Me neither,' Miss Jones concurred.

It was hardly surprising that, some time later on, Mr. Vint, the headmaster, cornered my parents after an end of term carol service held in the local parish church. Where did I get my hair colour from? He always pretended to warm his hands over my golden curls, as though they were a glowing fire. Anxiously, I looked up at my parents, detecting the awkward silence.

'Oh, she gets that from me,' Dad jumped in.

Mum shifted from one foot to the other, in wordless acquiescence.

I couldn't be sure if my dad did once have hair the same shade as mine. It was darkish at that time, as I recall, and specks of grey had started to appear along with a balding patch on top of his head. There were no past photographs to prove otherwise and even if there had been, they'd have been in black and white. But there was no way I'd have got it from him in any case.

You see, by then, I was in on the secret, and I knew my parents had been caught out. It was they who were guilty, not me. A lie, constructed in haste to save the situation. But why did the situation need saving? Why was it so shameful?

Dad was a Commander in the Royal Navy, having received fast promotion during the war. From Portsmouth, he'd joined up as a ship's stoker, aged fourteen. I was proud of the three gold rings he bore on the sleeves of his uniform, and I can recall the day not long after he'd retired from the 'Senior Service', as it was known, when the uniform was taken out of mothballs and he went to Buckingham Palace with Mum to be awarded the MBE. I was four.

I was proud of Mum, too. She'd trained as a physiotherapist, a pioneering profession in those days. In her thirties when war broke out, she'd returned home to look after her parents, and became head of department in a local hospital. When she and Dad married in 1947, they each had history. Their baggage, combined, was heavy.

Every night, throughout my childhood, while I lay in bed in the room above our lounge, Dad would sit down at the upright piano bought with his naval war gratuity, and play me to sleep. Gershwin and Cole Porter numbers, Rachmaninov, Debussy, all self-taught. In the daytime, he'd sit me on his lap and teach me chords to accompany simple melodies.

My favourite pieces of music were the opening of Grieg's Piano Concerto and Borodin's famous 'Nocturne'. I'd heard them many times on 'Your Hundred Best Tunes', which we always listened to on Sundays when we returned from evening service at church. When not played live, music emanated from the wireless all the time at home. As soon as it came on in the morning I danced and danced around the house, until eventually Mum decided it was time for me to start ballet lessons.

Music, art and writing were some of the best things about my life back then, and yes, on the whole I was a happy child. But I'm not sure if I was happy or sad when, at six years of age, my parents told me the truth. Some of the truth. We were sitting around our drop-leaf table of dark oak, which had been left behind at the previous house we'd lived in by its former owner, an old lady who'd died. My parents lived in married quarters to begin with, and since Dad had lost his home and entire possessions – indeed, much more than that – during a Portsmouth bombing raid while away at sea, any furniture was welcome. We were having a meal around it when a different sort of bombshell was dropped. I was adopted.

At first, I didn't know what the word meant, and it was explained to me that, after all, they weren't my 'real' parents but had chosen me specially, having gone up to London to fetch me. They made it all sound rather grand, how I'd come from a big house in a place called Baker Street, where Sherlock Holmes lived. I discovered later that he was a fictional character, and in time began to wonder if the rest was fiction too. It was a satisfying story though, and I chose to believe it, or at least I talked myself into believing it.

I asked what had happened to my 'real' mummy. Mum told me that she'd died.

Just as I'd chosen to imagine myself coming from this magnificent townhouse somewhere in London, I began to weave a convenient little explanation for myself. I don't know where I picked it up from, but I guess I just put two and two together, assisted by the vivid imagination of teenage school pals.

I'd seen a television drama in which one of the female characters died in childbirth. It began to make sense; I'd been a tiny baby when my parents first had me in their care, I could tell this from a black and white photograph displayed in an old leather album they possessed. A family get-together on Mum's side: grandparents, parents, Aunt Verity and her daughter – my cousin Eva – who was also adopted. The little group were clustered together, arranged on and around a garden seat in Aunt Astrid's back garden in Surrey. If my 'real' mother had died, it seemed that she'd given her life for mine.

I have recently asked myself why I never wondered about my 'real' father. Was the subconscious in some way protecting me from something that deep down inside I preferred not to contemplate? That something, which, at an organic level, I already knew?

To survive, as a child, I'd added to my story. Grief-stricken over the death of his wife, he couldn't bear to keep me. I would remind him of a painful time, so he'd chosen instead to give me up for adoption. In return, I never entertained the thought that he might be still alive. It was as if he too had died.

But I didn't then know what I know now. The power of DNA, the need to blot out certain knowledge that exists deep down within the human psyche.

2

The Search Begins

Those childhood thoughts and memories, how they grip me still! And how they gripped me that January morning in 2009. I leapt out of bed, grabbed my dressing gown, pulled it on as I rushed to the computer instead of heading to my apartment kitchen to make the usual cup of tea. I couldn't waste a minute further – put off that thing I'd always one day meant to do. Now it seemed the moment had arrived with a sense of sudden and commanding urgency. Was it already too late?

I fired up the desktop, recalling an earlier attempt made some years ago to search for that missing piece of my life, the time before my parents had apparently fetched me from Baker Street in London. It was when Sarah, my old college friend, had started to construct her family tree by joining an ancestry site.

'I envy you being able to do that,' I said to her one day down the phone.

'You still could,' she replied.

'But I've no idea where to start!'

Sarah thought for a moment.

'What about the Citizen's Advice Bureau?'

Acting upon my friend's suggestion, I found the

number of a local office, dialled it and waited. The ring tone persisted for quite some time until I replaced the receiver, relieved in some ways not to have to proceed. My desire to find my past would have to wait, putting on hold the making of a family tree, a luxury many took for granted along with another one, that of knowing their own flesh and blood.

Seated at the desktop I googled *'searching for my roots'* and was instantly transported to an ancestry site. Trying again, this time I typed *'searching for birth parents'*, since it seemed the best way to take me to the kind of online organisation that might be able to help me. A list came up and I chose the first option: 'The British Association for Adoption and Fostering' (generally known as BAAF), since closed down.

A form appeared for me to type into. How weird my message must have sounded. A sixty year old woman – well nearly! – who, due to circumstances, had left things rather late. Brought up sharp by the passage of time, I wondered if they might be able to help me.

I stopped short. Help me with what exactly? Find birth parents at this stage? Most certainly not! One was likely to be dead, as for the other – well I'd never stopped to think about him. I needed to find my true identity, that was all, relate to something tangible, learn where I'd come from.

I completed the message, pressed send. To my surprise

a reply came quite quickly. Yes, they could request information from the Government Registry Office. But first they needed to know where I lived, since the information I sought could only percolate down to me through an adoption society in my region. Furthermore, I learned, I needed to be assigned a counsellor, as I'd been adopted before 1976, the year in which the laws were changed. Those adopted after this date had a choice in the matter. I was miffed to be honest; why would I need a counsellor to learn a few simple truths? And yet, what was I letting myself in for? The discovery that what I'd been told as a child was indeed a lie? That my biological mother perhaps hadn't died after all?

Sometime during my childhood, Dad told me about a place called Somerset House in London. Birth records were kept there, he said, and I'd imagined that stored among them were details of my own. Had he been giving me permission to go ahead, I wondered? The laws were indeed different back then; such information unobtainable, but my dad was a far-seeing man. Would not a golden-haired child, with parents whose hair was black, want to find out such things one day?

But the decision to discover what lay behind my adoption was also fuelled by cousin Eva. She was the only child of the youngest of Mum's two elder sisters. Aunt Verity, like Mum, had married late and couldn't have children, although Mum once said that her elder sister's marriage to Uncle Edward, a schoolmaster, had been one of convenience, not love. The separate divan beds they'd slept in next to one another were surely testament enough; I'd seen the two pieces of furniture, placed side by side, for myself.

I was staying with Eva, and her German husband Klaus, in the Rhineland town of Remagen where they'd lived ever since they'd got married. I'd been there once before with my parents, during a river cruise, as a teenager.

'Have you considered looking into your past?' my cousin demanded.

Her sharp blue eyes, beneath a halo of raven coloured locks, drilled into me; features so at odds with those of her parents, just as mine had been with my own. We'd shared our experiences as children, found solace in common ground. In a gesture of unity, the two of us had exchanged stories of intrusive busybody questions and remarks made by teachers, school friends and their parents.

My cousin appeared to be laying down the gauntlet, challenging me to follow her example. It was something I intended to do one day, I responded meekly. But not when Mum was alive, I wanted to add – then stopped myself, since Aunt Verity was also still in the land of the living, though far away.

'I was trying to find out the children's medical history,' Eva went on.

I contemplated her in silence. There was no doubt that the system had robbed us both of that facility, and there had been a number of times when I'd been asked by earnest doctors if 'x', 'y' or 'z' ran in the family, to which I'd replied that I had no idea, explaining why. It was an inconvenience, undoubtedly, but I also wondered if it had been an excuse. Eva and Klaus's son and daughter might well have been owed an explanation as to their genetic inheritance, I realised, and yet I suspected that at a deeper level there existed an incurable curiosity on my cousin's part.

As Eva's story poured forth, I could see that the latter had prevailed. An adoption agency advised her to write a letter to her biological mother, who she'd managed to track down by a bit of sleuthing, having discovered her name. The result of this exercise provided the biggest slap in the face that someone in Eva's – my – position, risked facing. Rejection. Not once, but twice.

The woman had married, raised a family of four in a remote Welsh village. Eva's half-brothers and sisters. Now there were copious grandchildren. Eva's biological mother had been sent away to give birth, as unmarried women in her position often were in those days. She'd called her baby daughter Caroline. And she'd refused to name the father. My mind wandered for a moment. Had he been the local schoolmaster or the vicar? Or a member of the landed gentry, perhaps? Someone with a reputation to keep, who'd paid for silence?

Not content with this result, Eva had dragged a less than enthusiastic Klaus away on holiday to that very part of Wales and located the woman's house. Parking outside, her protesting husband had wandered off to look at the local sights, leaving Eva in the passenger seat. At that moment a woman opened the front door of the house and marched down the garden path. She had raven coloured hair, flecked with greying streaks, her features like Eva's. The woman opened the garden gate, stepped into the street and walked straight past.

'Be warned,' Eva's message seemed to say.

But now, despite the risks, I had to respond to that call to arms, listen to the voice in my head which had propelled me out of bed.

'You must start your search.'

I had no children, my past had seen to that. The belief that my own biological mother had died giving birth to me was so deeply embedded that I'd shied away from meaningful relationships when younger. Unattainable, unreliable men had been the name of the game. And, after receiving the reply from BAAF, I pondered the similarities and the differences that lay between me and Eva. I cared little for my own medical history, but now, confronted by the voice, I found myself desiring more than ever the knowledge of my own flesh and blood, so far denied me. Poised between the past, the present and the future, I stood at a cross-roads where, if I failed to heed the message, I could drift into a zone of dissatisfaction, of unfinished business, when things might one day prove to be too late.

And soon I'd be semi-retired, a time when no more school teaching loomed; instead, a handful of well motivated piano pupils who I taught at home. Full retirement wasn't something I could contemplate in any case, since music, along with writing, was my life. No babysitting of grandchildren, celebration of wedding anniversaries, trips to stately homes and gardens, copious 'aways' like some of my friends were enjoying. Sometimes I envied them – I really did – but I was driven by a different desire, one that had seeded itself in the environment in which I'd grown up.

For me it was about filling my days with creative pursuits: storytelling, writing music, teaching. An investment in the future, the shaping of happy human beings, bestowing upon them a gift for life. It was my passion, instilled into me as a child, encouraged and supported by my parents. And it was what I was born to do, to communicate this way, of that I was convinced, and I couldn't help but wonder from where it had come.

Was it nature, or nurture? A bit of both, or neither? I had often pondered this, especially at the times when Mum sat listening to me playing the piano, just as she'd listened to Dad all those years before. How she'd loved it; she could even name all the different styles and the composers. She hadn't learned to play herself, just imbibed music as one might a particularly good vintage of wine.

Occasionally, Mum would refer to my adoption, once I was well into adulthood. Not outright, but in oblique ways.

'At least you won't inherit that,' she'd say with an air of vagueness, when someone in the family – her blood family – contracted something nasty. Like Aunt Astrid's lung cancer, assisted in advancement by years of chain smoking. Or Granny Tanner's senile dementia, which had started to affect Aunt Verity. It had started to affect Mum too, the signs were evident and indeed she could discern it.

'Heaven only knows what *I've* inherited,' I once muttered in response.

She stared at me in silence, for she knew there was nothing she could say to me.

'My daughter's adopted,' she'd tell the nursing home matron, once in private care, after the dementia became so bad she couldn't remain at home. Wild imaginings seized hold of her, gnarled the pathways of her mind, blended the imagined with the real, the real with the imagined. Fears contained within her former self, about a child who long ago she very nearly lost –

was now convinced she'd lost again.

'Julie's run away – call the police!'

3

Family Ties

I'd waited so long to begin my investigations, ever since that day in January 1995, Dad's birthday. It was as if Mum had chosen the date in which to leave this world especially, joining at last her beloved James. She'd spent the last two years of her life in the care home, it was time to go.

The place had been recommended to me by a friend and at first I arranged that she went there on respite prior to Christmas. It was expensive but with the state and physiotherapy pensions, plus a naval widow's pension, we just about managed. I was determined to put her somewhere comfortable; the local state care homes were dreadful and she deserved better. When, after the respite period was up, the care home owner told me that Mum needed full time attention – either there or elsewhere – I jumped for joy. At last someone in authority had seen for themselves what she could be like when she wasn't 'presenting well'. I just couldn't cope anymore, was heading for a breakdown.

The dementia had begun insidiously, unrecognised at first as such. Subconsciously denied, there were times of huge frustration on my part when I returned from a tiring day of school teaching to discover yet another irrational piece of behaviour manifesting itself. Like 'the melon disaster' as I now call it. We'd devoured two slices the day before, yet when I looked in the fridge the remains were nowhere to be seen.

It was there yesterday – I was certain of it! I shot accusingly. Mum stared at me blankly, claimed to know nothing. Perhaps it was I who was going mad? I thought, as my eyes raked the fridge's almost empty shelves.

Then I saw it, on the lowest one, the carton of ice-cream I'd also purchased and opened the day before, cardboard soggy with gooey contents which had spilled out of the ripped-open container. The mixture oozed forth in a rivulet of melted vanilla down from the shelf onto the glass top above the vegetable drawer. From there it dripped further, finding its way inside. Angrily I stood up, flung open the door to the freezer compartment. There it lay, the half-eaten melon, yellow skin, pale green-white flesh and exposed beige coloured pips covered in the thinnest layer of frost crystals, ruined.

Aside from the incident with the melon, there were others, which, thrust together one after the other, began to mount up into a major situation of greatly worrying proportions. On one such occasion I found the nice electrician, who had supplied Mum with a new washing machine several years previously, standing in the kitchen wielding a mop. The floor was awash, since the machine did not, back then, have a safety lock. Obligingly – for he was indeed a nice man – he periodically squeezed the mop into a plastic bucket as, bit by bit, the water disappeared, while I stood on the threshold, aghast.

It hadn't been the first time he'd been called out to attend to the apparently recalcitrant machine. Until then it had behaved itself impeccably since the day of its delivery, so I'd believed. However it was the third time that month he'd been phoned by my mum, he told me, holding my bewildered gaze with steady eyes. They challenged me, albeit politely, as he explained matters, sotto voce. Mum had stopped the machine each time because she was sure it had broken down, when in fact it had reached a normal lull in its cycle. The drum full of water, frothy with soap suds, she'd opened the door and flooded the floor.

Equally serious issues began to emerge, gleaned from neighbours who, uncomfortable, had refrained from telling me that Mum had taken to wandering around the neighbourhood for days on end, claiming that there was no food in the house and that I'd vanished. Neither fact was true, and it was only when Mum was in the home on respite, mental confusion finally endorsed, that they dared to mention it. And there'd been the embarrassment of her phone calls to the school, when the office staff were forced to divulge with apologetic pity Mum's fantasies over my imagined disappearance.

That she had lost her mind was a tragedy. That I had to put her in a home at all was an even greater one. A professional woman, intelligent, well educated, exceptionally versed in current affairs. That she was my mum made it even worse. I adored her, felt that she'd been torn from me in both mind and body. And the fact that I was adopted made it all the more brutal. Destiny, which originally brought us together, had, all of a sudden, driven us cruelly asunder.

I owed her something, reflected in my almost daily visits to the home after school and at weekends, haunted by the thought that as a young baby I'd very nearly died. Mum had told me about it years before, how I'd vomited repeatedly and become seriously dehydrated. How Aunt Astrid – a senior doctor at the Ministry of Health – had sent along specialists to take a look at me. How they couldn't figure out what was the matter. It was an irony therefore, I couldn't help but muse, that my aunt had been in charge of maternity welfare during the war, responsible for introducing cod liver oil, dried milk and orange juice for babies into the country. With everything else ruled out, it was Mum who worked out the cause. Yes – the orange juice, I suffered from acidosis. She'd saved my life, and I guess in more ways than one. I wanted to make hers, in its final stages, as comfortable as possible, even if it meant a form of institutionalised incarceration.

* * *

But the residential care home had its limitations, too many freedoms where dementia sufferers were concerned. The freedom to wander along the main road, where Mum had been spotted by a member of staff on their way to work, zigzagging from side to side amongst the traffic. The freedom to meander into a local bank, even attempting to open an account there. On one such outing she had ended up in a petrol station, sat herself down and engaged in a friendly chat with the owner who, finally ascertaining where she was from, called a cab. There were even times when she rolled up outside the home in the back of a police car.

With Aunt Verity in a nursing home suffering from a similar condition which – yes – seemed to run in that family, the plan was to bring Mum back to her place of birth, put her in the same accommodation as her sister, while I'd get a job nearby. The latter happened first. But just as I was about to arrange the former, Mum fell down the main staircase in the home down south and ended up in hospital. She'd had a heart attack. I was up and down the country, sick with worry. I'd got another, permanent, job in the pipeline, as head of department in a convent school a friend of mine taught at, near the area where I'd previously lived. I was all set to go for an interview and fling in my temporary post. Things weren't working out at all. Then, early one morning, I phoned the hospital, as I had done each previous day, to ask how

Mum was.

'You do mean Mrs. Lillian Wetherby don't you?' a hesitant female voice – that of a duty nurse – ventured.

I assured her that I did. I'd spoken to the nurse before, and I sensed that she hoped I was somebody else, enquiring about somebody else. Was there another Mrs. Wetherby on the same ward perhaps? With a rampant flu epidemic doing the rounds, it wasn't beyond the bounds of possibility that two persons of the same name were confined to the same geriatric ward at the very same time. I prayed it was so, that the newfound seriousness in the nurse's familiar voice referred to Mum's possible namesake.

A heavy silence fell.

'I'll pass you on to the consultant,' she finally replied, her voice flat.

I'd also spoken to him before, a foreign sounding gentleman, Indian perhaps. Always kindly and upbeat, he spoke the words I'd dreaded: Mrs. Wetherby – yes – Mrs. Lillian Wetherby – my mother, had just that minute collapsed and passed away. He was really very sorry.

That evening, as I sat in a coffee shop, I heard yet another voice, telling me to stay. Hers.

The years rolled by and I became self-employed. There was a lot to do setting up my own business; a lot of risk taking, a lot of moving and a lot of hard work.

And I needed space, a respectable amount of time in which to pay homage to both my parents, because although Mum had outlived Dad by twenty-eight years, I owed it to them both not to muddy the waters by getting at the truth too soon. I was scared of finding out that I'd been lied to, and I was scared of finding a brick wall. No-one alive after all, or if they were, they wouldn't want anything to do with me. And the thing I had to some extent learned, and would learn even more, was that adoptees carry inside of them a great sense of rejection. It is laid down before birth and covered by the big white lies told after it.

But in 2009 I had other things to think about and look forward to. A further visit to see Eva and Klaus in Remagen, this time for a family reunion they were organising in order to celebrate various significant birthdays, my own included. Their son and daughter and other relatives would be attending, as well as relatives on Klaus's side of the family.

It was a place I'd already visited, aged fourteen, when my parents took me on the river cruise, in a country that most people frowned upon, even in the 1960s. But they'd wanted me to see it all, to absorb the scenery, history and culture that stretched far into the past, centuries before the horrors of the first and second world wars. They had vision, my parents, even greater than I realised.

4

The End of 'Life: Part One'

The family reunion: times spent on café terraces eating cake and drinking coffee. Dappled late July sunshine lighting up the green-blue waters of the Rhine, barges with cargoes of timber, coal and rows of closely stacked containers ploughing back and forth between Rotterdam and Basel. Warm evenings passed in a haze of wine and beer in local taverns, strolls through the town of Remagen. The circular twin towers of dark grey stone, each pair on either bank, facing one another across the river, all that remained of the Ludendorff Bridge destroyed in 1945 at the end of the war. And the Peace Museum, which occupied the ones on the Remagen side. Evocation of bittersweet memories.

A boat trip further downstream conveyed us one day to Königswinter on the opposite western bank. Boarding a crowded road train, we sat on hard wooden seats, elbow to elbow, thigh to thigh, riding through narrow cobbled streets, past pavement cafés and picturesque medieval timbered buildings. Eva, Klaus, their married son and single daughter, grandchildren, German cousins on Klaus's side, and me, bunched close.

Next, upwards, on another train equally packed with tourists; it clung to a steep cogwheel railway.

Transported to the summit of the Drachenfels, we made for a lookout point affording wide panoramic views. I remembered it. Far below us the glistening river cut through the Rhineland plateau landscape, flowing lazily onwards and stretching out of sight, to the distant horizon, past places I knew that lay beyond Remagen. Linz-am-Rhein, Boppard, Rudesheim. Narrow villages embracing steep-sided banks, tiny clustered vineyards barely visible to the naked eye, fairy tale castles, distant trains snaking along the river's edge. The Lorelei Rock. They haunted me – with happiness, sadness, and regret.

A dinner with speeches crowned the weekend celebrations. That, and the extra large mocha birthday cake. It was served up one teatime to celebrate three significant milestones – that of Klaus, five years older than me, a German cousin turning seventy, and mine. Never once did I mention that I'd started my search. I didn't dare.

Distracted, I'd almost forgotten the meeting with Angela – my newly appointed counsellor – the Friday after my return, forgetting even more the reason for it. It was a sunny afternoon in early August when I rolled up at the sturdy, red brick gabled townhouse, entering the building through an imposing pillared porch with a shiny brass door knocker. Arriving early, I was left to sit with a cup of coffee and a magazine in the interview room, at a large circular table of pale wood. On the far side was a box of tissues; I couldn't help thinking that it looked a bit odd, just lying there.

From next door, yelps of delight seeped through the walls – encouraging whooping noises from adults and children. I wondered what could possibly be going on in there. Some kind of bonding process I guessed, remembering how children, removed from dysfunctional backgrounds, were much older these days when they were put up for adoption. There had been big social changes since the time of my own; back then, babies were relinquished by middle class people in order to avoid being shunned by society. But hadn't my parents got married? Surely it was death that had parted us? Grown strong in the re-telling, this story still held me in its clutches. Was it really true?

Angela arrived at the appointed hour. From the moment she came into the room, I felt in safe hands. Tall with fairish hair, straight and bobbed, she was near my age, I guessed, calm and efficient. We chatted for a while and talked of possible next steps should I choose to take things forward with the investigation process. I imagined it to be just a matter of doing some ancestry research, then putting the matter finally to rest, I said. Secretly, I had started to hope for something more.

There was a yellow sheet of A4-sized paper lying face down on the table, next to the tissues. I hadn't noticed it until later on in the interview, when it just appeared, surreptitiously.

'Do I get to know my name at birth today?' I broached, recalling the process outlined in some correspondence received from the Government Registry Office in Southport, Lancashire. Somerset House, now an arts centre, no longer held public records, I'd discovered. Angela replied in the affirmative, leaned forward and deftly steered the yellow sheet towards me. I turned it over.

My world changed forever, just then, life divided into two parts. The first, from as far back as I can remember, a time when I lay outdoors in my pram. And the second, which began from that moment in the present, seated at the circular pale wooden table. Nothing would ever be the same again – I would never be the same again.

It was the name my eyes flew to. Rose Keller. Rose? Did I feel like a Rose? And there was so much to take in. Especially my family name.

'Keller. That's German, isn't it?'

Angela thought it had sounded interesting. Keller was German for cellar, that much I knew from my self-taught attempts at the language. But there were other disturbing factors – principally my place of birth in Guildford. Aunt Astrid had lived on the outskirts of Surrey's county town and had known several doctors who worked as general practitioners in the area. I'd always thought I was born in London; that's what it said in my passport.

After the revelation of my adoptive status, when it was delivered over the oak drop-leaf table that lunch time, all those years ago, I first assumed I'd been born in Baker Street. Later I became convinced that the place was a children's home, visualising rows of cots with screaming babies all calling for the attention of prospective parents as they strolled around the room. 'Choose me! Choose me!' So to have this theory smashed in one fell swoop was disquieting, all the more because I had a kind of 'Aha!' moment, when everything made sense and clicked into place. It felt scary, yet right, at one and the same time.

I told Angela about the disparity of information – that this discovery underlined something I'd always sensed. Aunt Astrid was behind my adoption; it explained the proprietorial rights she appeared to have exercised over me.

There were the stories. How, after the war, Mum left her hometown in the North and took a physiotherapy job based in Winchester. Living in digs for a while, she shared a meal table with naval officers. Each morning there was a queue for the only bathroom while the men shaved, so she found herself a flat and moved out. It wasn't long before one of the officers knocked on the front door. My dad.

It also wasn't long before the pair became engaged;

the war-torn couple weren't hanging around – you knew a good thing when you saw it. Aunt Astrid turned up at the engagement dinner, she gushingly informed me one evening, when, as a teenager, I'd had the misfortune to stay with her alone. This was a situation that my mum had tried, successfully up until then, to avoid. Had she – my aunt – really done that? I queried, somewhat surprised. Of course she had, she'd paid the bill – how could she possibly forget? – came the indignant retort.

Seated with my parents round the oak drop-leaf table one lunchtime after my return home, I relayed this information. My dad, normally mild-mannered, shook with suppressed rage. Quietly the anger rumbled inside him, nearing explosion point, before me. Lies, all lies!

Years later, after Aunt Astrid's demise, Mum told me how my aunt, prior to the wedding, managed to get herself invited to a function at the Admiralty, while never mentioning it beforehand.

It came to me then, at the dawning of 'Life: Part Two' – Aunt Astrid was in love with Dad. Little wonder she'd tried to stop my parents from getting married. Unsuccessful, she'd reaped pleasure in pulling strings and taking credit for it. In her medical capacity she'd told Mum not to go on trying for a child: it would likely be born with Down's syndrome, as she was far too old. It made perfect sense – of course it did – for Aunt Astrid to secure one for my parents. Me.

5

Digging up the Past

During the early days of 'Life: Part Two' I stared at myself in the mirror, repeated the name over and over. Rose Keller. I rather liked it, it had a ring to it. Perhaps I could change my name by deed poll [illegible] perhaps not. Aside from all the complicated paperwork involved, which spilled over into changing details on bank accounts and other tiresome matters, there was the question of my passport. Julie Wetherby had been born in London – metaphorically – to my adoptive parents. Rose Keller hadn't. No: it was far too convoluted, and best left alone. I was playing games with myself. But what if things had been otherwise? What if I'd become someone else?

Things could have been different, very different, I'd discovered. And I hadn't liked what I'd found. On that yellow sheet of A4 paper not only had my name and place of birth been revealed, but also the identity of my biological mother. Joyce Keller. A midwife.

Immediately I returned to the fount of all knowledge, the internet, and joined an ancestry site. In so doing I played detective. I discovered that the Kellers had settled in the Midlands at the end of the nineteenth century. And, much to my astonishment, I also learned that my biological great grandparents hailed from the Rhineland town of Remagen.

Yes – the place where cousin Eva lived and where my adoptive family's recent reunion was held. The place I'd once been to with my parents. Where before I'd experienced mild goosebumps, now the hairs stood up on the back of my neck and the chills swept over me. Impressionable memories of a distant Rhineland cruise were reawakened – a vision of a swastika daubed in red paint on a wall reminding my parents of things on which, even back then, I sensed they preferred not to dwell. And recollections of things they did voice, such as the affluence of a nation that had leapt ahead of Britain, seen in the shops and streets of Cologne and Bonn. And there was a vision of the Lorelei Rock approaching on the starboard bow, shrouded in ghostly mist, invoking the legend of Wagnerian sailors lured to their deaths by a mermaid.

'Like Beachy Head on a rainy day,' a crew member had observed wryly.

I shivered.

My discovery was greatly assisted by someone I calculated to be a third cousin, married to an American and living in Boston. Maggie, as she was called, had instigated some research on the same website ten years earlier. It appeared that she was descended from a younger daughter of the Keller great grandparents; there'd been fifteen of them in total! My grandfather – Robert Keller – was a much older brother.

Maggie, the narrative thread indicated, had been contacted by some other Keller descendants also living in the States. Claiming Rhineland origins, their forefathers emigrated to the Midwest about the time our great grandparents arrived in England. This distant branch of the family, contributing to Maggie's posting soon after its inception, emitted gloomy signals. According to one such American Keller, the original family had moved away from the Remagen area, and subsequent wartime atrocities, including the deliberate bombing of civilian populations in the second world war, rendered finding any descendants of the remaining branch of the Keller family there, unlikely.

I decided to make contact with the third cousin through an e-mail link on the site. My message explained how I'd only recently found out that I'd been born to a Joyce Keller sixty years ago and was given up for adoption as a baby. I'd set a veritable cat amongst the pigeons: her ancestry board posting now revealed a new family scandal.

I was interested in learning anything at all about my biological roots, I said. Her rapid reply contained attachments. Black and white photographs of my great grandparents on their wedding day; young, frightened, newly arrived in a foreign land, my grandmother's slim waist concealing the child she carried. And the groom, handsome and moustached, compelled to seek his fortune away from the fatherland. There was a photo of tombstones in an English churchyard where the pair of them were buried, and a photograph taken in the 1900s – a large family grouping, younger boys and girls in sailor suits, elder siblings in baggy shapeless clothes.

I printed off the photographs and studied the family grouping more carefully. Everyone wore solemn expressions, including my great grandmother, who, despite giving birth to so many offspring, still looked remarkably good, even with her severe, matriarchal countenance. Somewhere amongst them all was my grandfather. Where before I'd yearned to see just one blood relative, I was now confronted by seventeen.

The cousin informed me that she'd wondered about my birth when doing her research. She had reason to. Like her, I'd uncovered, on the website, not just one skeleton, but two. Apart from Rose, registered in 1949, there was another, Brenda, recorded the following year. Both were born to a woman whose maiden name was Keller. If it was the same Keller, of course. But given the months in which we'd been recorded, I had a sneaking suspicion that it was. Too much of a coincidence otherwise, and the births were certainly biologically possible.

In the days that followed my first visit to the adoption society – week one of 'Life: Part Two' – I became wedded to the computer. Unlike humans, ancestry records, although not always exact, don't lie. There, in black and white, is the stark truth, human nakedness displayed in print, for anyone at all interested to see. Players assembled on a public stage, when once they'd believed their actions took place in secret, curtains drawn.

Not that this information is easy to access. For a start, it's quite expensive to belong to an ancestry site. One can join free for several weeks, but after that a hefty annual subscription kicks in. By then I was hooked, of course, and before the free time was up, I knew my research had only just begun. For one thing, I wanted to assemble that much longed-for family tree, whose flaking timber I'd stumbled upon at last.

For someone like me, it costs to access greater details of their birth, background and original identity. And you have to know what you're looking for. This can only be done with the correct information to hand. Something that is a natural birthright must be purchased, and, as I was to discover, even then there is no guarantee that the desired information and outcome will be forthcoming. The way was paved with potholes.

I'd also had to pay to obtain my original birth certificate, one of the first things I did when given several forms to fill out at the initial meeting with Angela. It was a good deal nicer than the tacky little piece of paper I'd been obliged to produce from time to time during 'Life: Part One.' On one particularly mortifying occasion, when I'd just turned twenty, I was called up by potential part time employers to explain, in front of other candidates, why my place of birth wasn't recorded on it. I guess the powers that be had never seen anything so rudimentary, while I, myself, was entirely ignorant of the fact that normal birth certificates didn't look at all like mine. The certificate in question was even more vague than my passport, since it just declared that I'd been born in England.

Worse still, when obliged to explain to my interrogators that I was born in London but didn't know where exactly because I was adopted, they made ugly faces.

'Oh,' they said, in withering tones.

6

A Matter of Life and Death

'Bugger Rose Keller!' I spat one morning, having heaved myself out of bed for another day of 'Life: Part Two'. There she was again, staring at me in the mirror. I was obsessed by her. By Joyce Keller too, alive when I'd supposed her to be dead. Every single day of 'Life: Part One', she'd been somewhere, doing something, leading a parallel existence. The idea was hideous. History rewritten in a matter of days.

After discovering the Keller family from the ancestry site, I began to focus on just one member, her. Had she given birth to another? This time I called up the Government Registry Office at Southport and ordered copies of Brenda's birth certificate (for a fee, naturally!), just to learn whether she was a sister – half, or full. And because I wanted the information as soon as possible, I forked out even more to have them sent by express delivery.

The certificates arrived several days later, revealing what in my heart I already knew. Brenda was indeed Joyce Keller's daughter, and she – Joyce – a single mother. We were stamped with that dreaded unwritten word. Illegitimate. I once asked Mum what it meant and she'd got all flustered when trying to explain that someone had been born 'illegally'. At the time, I hadn't been – of course! – my parents were married. On another occasion I'd mentioned the word 'bastard', only to be instantly reprimanded.

'Don't swear, Julie!'

The ancestry site findings exposed Joyce at her worst as far as I was concerned. I discovered that she was born in 1922, and traced her to a marriage registration in 1951, when she became espoused to a certain Desmond Gabbitas. A nasty little thought was lurking at the back of my mind. And after further searching, my worst suspicions were confirmed. Brenda Keller had become Brenda Gabbitas, a fact made visible on the internet, since in 1981 she'd married a gentleman with a Spanish-sounding name.

I was enraged! Why had Brenda been kept, when I'd been given away? Why had the far right-hand column of her birth certificate not borne the same identical word as in mine? – *'Adopted'*.

I shifted my line of enquiry to Joyce's husband, and found his death registered in 1985. A bit of delving revealed the Gabbitasses to be professional people who enjoyed a privileged lifestyle. Desmond, a GP, had been educated at an English public school and was a few years older than Joyce. Moreover, he'd been married twice before, within the space of five years. The first marriage had taken place during wartime and I was unable to find any evidence of children. The second occurred in 1945, after demob. There appeared to be no children from this union either.

Had Desmond been seeing Joyce during his second marriage, sowing his wild oats with her? It seemed likely, since I found that his wife of that time also remarried, in 1952, and had later given birth to a daughter. I was sure that Desmond Gabbitas was our father, the pieces fitted together.

I returned to the adoption society a week after my first visit, armed with information. For a start I'd reconstructed the ever spreading Keller family tree, encompassing four generations. I also took the copy of Brenda's birth certificate, to show Angela.

In a way, I'd achieved what I'd wanted. Firstly to find out who I was at birth, and secondly to be able to make a family tree, even if the members of it meant nothing to me in reality. I'd never met my grandparents, aunts, uncles, or cousins, or my sister. Most of them probably didn't even know I existed. Apart from one, the third cousin on the ancestry site, and Joyce of course. It wasn't, after all, such a satisfying experience.

So what was I left with? The chilling notion that Joyce Keller had not only lived after I was born, but that she might still be alive. And there was another thought. I'd calculated that Joyce was eighty-seven, the same age as Mum when she'd died fourteen years earlier. Time was of the essence.

I wasn't even sure that I wanted to meet Joyce. I didn't feel particularly well disposed towards her. But yes – I was curious. How to start, then?

Angela suggested I begin my search at Joyce's last known address, recorded four years previously on the electoral roll. I'd managed to track it down through the online 192 directory enquiries site – another purchase!

The next task, a somewhat morbid one, was to establish whether Joyce was still alive. It entailed looking up information on a website and extracting contact details for three different areas of the county where death records were kept. Two out of the three people I spoke to over the phone were helpful when I explained why I was asking, but one, suspicious of me, had to defer to his boss in order to pass on the information I wanted. No-one by the name of Joyce Gabbitas had been registered.

She could of course have moved elsewhere and, if so, that was going to make the next part of my investigation even more difficult, if not impossible. But I was ready to persevere with the required step: to obtain the address and telephone number of social services in the county where Joyce had last lived. It was worth a try.

After several false starts, I managed to track down the adoption arm of the relevant social services department. I was put through to a lady called Diane. She listened with some sympathy to my story, one of desperation to find my eighty-seven-year old mother who I hoped was still alive.

Wasn't it years ago that she'd given me up? she argued. It was probably a closed chapter in her mind, something that had been dealt with long ago. Why trouble an elderly lady with such disturbing news at this stage? Implicit in that were doubts as to my motives. I was aware it might be so, and although nothing was said along those lines at that point, I knew what would be present in Diane's mind, and in the minds of anyone involved in the nitty gritty process of enabling me to trace my birth mother: could I be after money?

I was angry. Not on the phone, not to Diane; that wouldn't have got me anywhere. But deep down inside. Angry that the wheels of bureaucracy could grind to a halt, and block my path to attain what was rightfully mine. It was out of her hands, Diane told me, there was nothing further she could do. *Was prepared to do*, she might have added. But surely it was down to Joyce, to decide whether or not to take it any further? At least she should be given the chance. That is, if she really was still alive. What was I to do?

7

Legal Jargon

Angela came to the rescue. First she contacted Diane, ascertaining that the route to finding Joyce was likely to be blocked. An untimely reminder was issued: let it not be forgotten that the parties were, back then, assured that circumstances leading to the relinquishment of a baby in a court of law were kept private. Forever.

The past locked away, those involved had been free to invent the present and the future. How I knew it, how deeply drilled such knowledge was into my consciousness. How thoroughly did I understand that their beliefs and subsequent whitewashing of the truth, embedded in society and the legal system representing it, fell short of humanity.

Collectively, they failed to understand that the Julie Wetherbys of this world needed to meet the Rose Kellers. They failed to appreciate the moral right to do so, the necessity to fit together the missing puzzle pieces belonging to each of these identities. And they failed to realise how each needed to brood and grieve for the other, for what might have been, for what had been.

But with one single move, Angela overrode both Diane and the social services department, by contacting the county solicitor. An empathetic lady, she declared that it was down to the interpretation of the law. Thus, with great reluctance I suspect, Diane went into action, and dragged her heels in so doing.

This was just one side of the coin. In my zealousness to send away the two forms Angela had given me at the first interview, one requesting my birth certificate, I hadn't anticipated the kind of response to the other. Dutifully filled out, I'd posted it to the Juvenile Court where I'd been adopted. Involved as I was with my own online findings, I'd failed to take on board what I was actually requesting, simply assuming that it was a matter of being given some kind of official recognition to support the next stage of my search. How wrong I was.

A letter from the court judge arrived on the doormat a few weeks after the social services people were contacted. One of us, Angela or myself, would need to attend a court hearing, in order to make a case for the release of my adoption file. I had no idea that such a thing existed, or that information pertinent to my past could be withheld.

The county solicitor's views on legal interpretation did not, unfortunately, spread to the willing handing over of documentation that was surely of more relevance to me than to present day law court officials. Besides, the presiding members of this particular law court were ignorant as to what was going on in the adjacent county regarding the search for my birth mother. Had they been aware of it, my request to view the file would most surely have led to rejection. With this information necessarily withheld, it was left to a judge in the juvenile court of my adoption to make a decision, with either my counsellor or myself present.

It would be Angela, we both agreed; I couldn't face the stress of attending the place where I'd been adopted, cap in hand, begging for my rights. A letter written was all that would be required of me. From communications with the clerk to the court, I had the distinct impression that the file might contain information of an upsetting nature, possibly damaging to others as well as to myself. Since my parents had long passed on and Joyce might not even be alive, I still couldn't see why this should be so hush hush. Weren't we all living in a much enlightened age, where social attitudes had changed? The file was my hidden past story, mine alone, and I wanted it.

I wrote the letter, assuring the judge I was of sound mind, and that I got on with other adoptive relatives. Why – we'd even met for a shared birthday reunion in Germany during the summer! I positively grovelled, in order to prove that I was worthy to receive the information. I explained that I'd reached a stage in my life, a watershed, was taking stock and wished to fill in some gaps that had, until now, eluded me. No-one else need ever see the file, I undertook, it was for my eyes only, and those of my counsellor. And given the arena in which I was adopted, I dwelt upon the fact that my birth had taken place in the aftermath of the war, a time when life was hard, and that allowances were made.

I found the court on Google Maps, a modern two storeyed building of red brick, with a car park full of vehicles and overlooked by a high-rise block of flats. How I would have hated going there! I could imagine Angela with her usual efficiency, suited and smart, ushered into a modern faceless courtroom, empty except for a clerk dressed in black, and a bewigged judge installed on a throne-like, high-backed chair behind a long table. Angela seating herself down in front of him, then cross-examined as to the contents of my letter. A legal pronouncement made in my favour would follow, and a copy of my file be handed over by the clerk, before the judicial audience was rounded off by a shaking of hands.

The outcome to my hopes met, as I'd imagined, Angela duly returned with the file. A letter then arrived addressed to myself from the clerk, signed by the judge. A long piece of impersonal jargon, it cited previous cases, decisions to release files made on various grounds of historical significance within a legal setting. The findings in the interview with Angela, as well as the information I'd provided in my letter, were also recorded. In short I was considered to be of mature outlook, and seeing that some of the persons mentioned in the file were likely to have passed away, the judge had decided to release the copy.

I'd been going through old photographs prior to my next visit to Angela. Tiny black and white ones, mounted on stiff dark pages, contained in the ancient leatherbound photograph album. There was one of me after my christening, in Mum's arms, my doting dad inspecting me with pride and joy. Among them – that photograph taken a few months earlier, in the summer of 1949, me a few weeks old in Aunt Astrid's back garden, outside Guildford. Leaning over the garden seat, smiling gaze fixed upon me, my aunt seemed to me to emulate, in suspect guise, a magical fairy godmother: *'Look what I've brought about,'* the expression suggested.

My dad, dressed in his naval uniform, stood at the other end of the row, frowning. Was he hating every minute of being at Aunt Astrid's? Or was it something else? The two of them bookended a gathering including, next to Dad, a cowed-looking Aunt Verity, abreast of Grandpa Tanner. Central, upright and sombre, he embodied the strict Edwardian gentleman; I was always somewhat frightened of him. He towered, as though he might once have been head of the family, alongside Mrs.Goody, Aunt Astrid's diminutive housekeeper, making her look even more so than ever.

In the front row sat dear old Granny Tanner, a smile on her face. Kind and sunny natured, a little servile to her husband, everyone loved her to bits. Beside her, raven-haired cousin Eva, perched on the edge of the seat complete with baby doll, not to be outdone by the live version to the other side of her, positioned on her mother's lap and the centre of attention.

I'd seen this photograph, scrutinised now with fresh eyes, so many times before. And I was soon to look at it again, knowing things of which I wasn't then aware.

8

The Blitz

I took the photograph album along, to show Angela, after she next called me. Together we sat at the circular table of pale wood, basking for a moment in the artificial tableau of tranquility that lay in front of us. I knew I was playing for time.

'This can't have been taken long after Joyce gave me up,' I said, while Angela pored over the family grouping. I'd concluded as much since I'd discovered online that my birth had been registered two weeks after the event. The photograph proclaimed summertime, even though dear old Granny Tanner was clothed, as always, in a black suit and high necked, pin tucked blouse adorned by a cameo brooch, her laced up leather boots reaching to the ankles. But my mum and two aunts wore lightweight dresses, as did cousin Eva. 'Surely they couldn't have adopted me in such a short time?' I pressed.

'You were being fostered then,' Angela replied quickly. I sensed my counsellor was preparing me for something of profound significance and as I focused again on the minute black and white scene, an unnerving realisation crept over me. The infant perched on Mum's lap was none other than Rose Keller. Instantly I was reminded of the purpose of this visit: to receive into my hands the copy of my adoption file, recently arrived.

It lay somewhere out of sight at first, although I'd noticed, when Angela entered the interview room, a bulky folder tucked beneath her arm. There was a shortage of available accommodation that day; I'd been squeezed into a small window of time and knew I'd taken up too much of it already. I was clinging to something, a desperate attempt to retain vestiges of an already teetering status quo.

A sharp knock at the door interrupted our contemplations. Angela jumped up and opened it. Someone was needing the room, someone senior by the looks of things. I felt sick. My counsellor stepped outside, whispered tones pulsated in the corridor. There was urgent business to be attended to, we weren't quite finished; I didn't need to hear the words.

Back immediately, Angela seated herself at the table and produced the file she'd brought in, placing it in the centre, just like that yellow A4 sheet of paper.

There were pages of it, contained within the folder. Documents with wording bashed out on an old-fashioned typewriter: forms, and letters. Some were handwritten. I turned back the upper covering of card, the letter of stiff, grey-blue Basildon Bond – a luxury back in those days – lying there on the top. The words stared up at me in dark blue ink, writing familiar from childhood. They cut through me, burst open my heart.

'I desire to adopt Rose Keller.' Signed James W. Wetherby, Commander RN.

He'd known my name, two worlds colliding in that one single sentence. The next instalment of 'Life: Part Two.'

Choked, I forced myself to turn the pages, held together by a treasury tag. It would take me ages to digest all this, get to grips with what the folder contained. But soon after my dad's letter, something else caught my eye. Another name. Charles Walton Dempsey. Typed. Underneath it, more dark blue ink; a bold signature against a statement undertaking to assist with the cost of keeping the said Rose Keller. Thoughts tore across my mind. Was he some kind of philanthropist who'd taken pity on me in my hour of need? Or was he something else?

'Who is this man?' I demanded, frantic to get at the truth. In that same moment I knew the answer and didn't want to hear it. 'Is he my father?' I added, in trepidation. Angela nodded. Putative father was the official term. Underneath the signature, a job description. But she was already enunciating it.

'A commercial traveller.'

Bang went all my imaginings about Desmond Gabbitas, the GP. I'd been kind of proud to have a father who was engaged in a respected profession. Instead, the vision of a one night stand in some sleazy little hotel room barged into my thoughts. An itinerant man passing through from time to time.

My mind raced on. Where did Desmond and Brenda fit into all of this? Perhaps I was Charles Walton Dempsey's daughter, while Brenda was Desmond's, in which case Joyce had been quick to get involved with another man soon after my birth. And even if Brenda was also Charles Dempsey's daughter, Joyce hadn't let the grass grow under her feet.

Angela shifted in her chair.

'I'm very sorry Julie, but as I explained, we don't have much time,' came her quiet warning.

I'd read it all later, I felt obliged to promise, desperate to steer my way as fast as possible through the mound of unfriendly literature surrounding my undiscovered past. It was best to do so at home, then contact her with my thoughts when ready, we both agreed.

I left the respectable, Victorian red-brick building perplexed and shocked. I understood why the court judge had been hesitant; there was so much to think about. Suddenly, I wasn't sure that I wanted to find Joyce at all. She'd suited herself, possibly continuing an affair with the man who'd fathered me, and yet had no intention of getting married. And then she'd fallen into the arms of another, who had.

At the oak drop-leaf table, I waded through the pages, trying to make sense of it all. Even today I've kept my word to the judge, and never shown a soul that file. I have no desire to do so, it's sacred. But much of the information I gleaned from it has mostly since been recounted to me by others, close to the story. And, as reckoned by the court judge, my adoptive parents, along with the biological grandparents also mentioned in the file, were indeed deceased.

I discovered quite soon that Charles Walton Dempsey had died back in 1979 – I'd looked him up on the ancestry site straightaway. Serendipitously, he was exactly the same age as my dad when he'd passed away before him, twelve years earlier. The former had died far from his hometown, and barely ten miles from where I was living at the time. Had I set eyes on him? Had he seen me? Had he tried looking for me, watching me, if only from a distance? It was three years after the adoption laws had changed, after all. Maybe he'd hired someone to find me. Or maybe it was just one more of those strange coincidences.

Over the months, Charles Dempsey's story gradually discharged its rancid contents, exuding a noxious concoction of divided loyalty, self-protection and fear. It stemmed from sources that, over time, were to elicit a poignant pause for reflection on my part, the need for a surreptitious flick of a handkerchief to wipe away tears that stung the corners of the eyes. It was like a moment spent before the grave of someone whose life has been a melange of yearning and regret, sometimes selfish, sometimes thoughtless. Someone who wants it all, yet cannot have it.

The war, 1940, the Blitz at its height. Still I can visualise the stray German Heinkel droning across a starlit sky, then silence, bomb doors opening. Next a sudden explosion in which the naked eighteen year old Charles is blown into the air amid shards of flying metal, glass and falling timber. Above him, twinkling stars shine through a hole in the roof. Darkness too, and choking smoke. And light: bright, then dim, then bright. It hadn't come from the stars, just flickers of gold and yellow, hissing and crackling. The house was on fire.

Every movement forward spelled pain. Downwards where the staircase had been, downwards over displaced planks of floorboard and rusty nails, tearing at flesh, remnants of carpet smacking at the face. The taste of dirt in the mouth, dust in the nostrils reaching down to the lungs, thick, heavy, acrid, from burning wood and powdered bricks. The sound of faint moans coming closer from below. Shouting too, outside. Neighbourhood dogs barking, torches illuminating the house silhouetted against a bright burning sky. His parents – my grandparents – though it doesn't seem right for me to own them, carried out on stretchers. And the clanging of an ambulance bell as the vehicle races in vain through the streets to the hospital.

The putative father's own father died as a result of

the air raid, that's what the file said. Like others, victims of another German bomb, in another town. In the very same year.

9

Curiouser and Curiouser

Ellen Dempsey, née Walton. My biological grandmother. Cold, distant, the antithesis of Granny Tanner. Widowed during the war and left with an adored only son – but one whom she threatened to disinherit if he dared to get engaged to Joyce. It was how the story appeared to go from the moment I first read the file from cover to cover, gathered further through the droplets of information that have since come my way.

Mrs Dempsey hadn't liked Joyce, that's what my birth mother told Margery Brownlow. Miss Brownlow was secretary of the Baker Street branch of the National Adoption Society; the place from where my parents claimed to have collected me – so that much was true, after all.

Miss Keller had brought her baby along with her, the file said, when Miss Brownlow visited the nursing home. Two week old Rose, seemingly perfect in every way, early glimmers of her mother's golden curls crowning her lily-white scalp. Encased within a wicker basket on loan from the home, she lay on the floor, gurgling gently, thrashing out the occasional limb, which beat more furiously as the conversation progressed.

A sensible woman, Miss Keller, practical yet sympathetic. Miss Brownlow asked if she was absolutely sure she that she wanted to give up her child. There was no choice, came the reply; the boyfriend's own mother was an invalid, in poor health, having already suffered a heart attack, and had lost her husband in a wartime bombing raid. The boyfriend could have married her, Miss Keller then claimed: none of this need be happening! But divided loyalties meant that he hadn't felt able to. Now he was adamant that his mother must not be put to any extra stress by the revelation of an illegitimate child. Absolutely not!

It would be Miss Keller's decision now, hers alone, Margery Brownlow warned. Did she really know what adoption involved? Did she truly realise that the signing of papers meant the relinquishment of all rights to Rose, that she would never be able to see her again? – Miss Keller knew that, yes.

Excuses were made, seemingly justifiable ones. Miss Keller had to work, there'd be no-one to look after her child, it was far better for Rose to go to a married couple who would love her. Did that mean Joyce hadn't felt that way? I wondered. A midwife by profession with personal feelings pushed aside, already she seemed incapable of the sort of love Mum had lavished upon me. It didn't suit her to get entangled, she must remove herself, fast, exonerated by doing what she felt was best for her child. That much was clear.

Her parents mustn't find out. *"They mustn't!"* she emphasised. They'd be most upset if they learned of Rose's existence, they shouldn't ever know about her.

Everyone else appeared to matter more to her, then, took precedence over her baby – me. Not least, herself. Careless in her liaison with Charles Dempsey, consumed with passion, thought for the consequences far from her mind, Rose seemed to be dispensable.

What of Brenda, then? I asked myself. In our mother's desperation to hand Rose – me – over to the adoption society, it was preposterous to think that Joyce had conceived another child with the same man. Had it been due to a sudden flash of regret and guilt, that she'd kept her? Brenda might, after all, be a full sister. More than ever I hoped not; rather, that she was the daughter of Desmond Gabbitas.

It was my desire to get to the root of this outrageous story that urged me on with my determination to try to find this woman, my birth mother. I was in too deep to give up now. It was multifaceted, and, apart from Angela, I alone had a seat in the auditorium to watch the hitherto hidden drama unfold before me.

The star of the show none other than myself, I was audience and performer rolled into one. Onstage – a passive, vulnerable commodity without a say in the matter, at the mercy of decisions made by grown-ups, the system and society. Offstage – an adult, equally vulnerable, shaken and horrified but, in this modern age, supported by a counsellor who listened.

The scene shifted from Joyce at the nursing home, to Joyce leaving Rose at the nursing home in the care of a wet nurse until suitable prospective parents came forward, while she returned to work. What a conjurer she was, disappearing off to a far-flung corner of the country, cleverly explaining away her absence. And somehow, I was to learn, she managed to take up with her boyfriend of seven years when she returned to her parents' address, the one she'd provided for the registration of Rose's birth.

Next – my adoptive parents. I returned once more to the old photograph's choreographed little tableau, arranged on and around the seat in Aunt Astrid's back garden. Rose – there she was again. She wasn't even yet a legally accepted member of the Wetherby-Tanner family.

Theatre lighting had transformed the scene; a tangible frailty now hung over the group, wreathed for the most part in smiles – hopeful, optimistic, yet anxious. I was drawn again to the furrowed brow of my usually happy, carefree dad. My 'joke father' as I used to call him. And to Aunt Astrid's visibly self-satisfied joy at the sight of me on Mum's lap.

Although my adoption couldn't be classed as private, since an organisation dealing in such matters was involved, I was more convinced than ever that my aunt had nonetheless been operating behind the scenes. I could hear the hushed conversations in corridors, muffled by closed consulting room doors, secretive calls transmitted down telephone lines. There was a child, perfect in every way, with golden hair, born to an unmarried mother (let's not be too fine upon the point!) and left in a first class nursing home in the depths of the home counties.

My parents had been offered another child by the society, but they wanted this one, Miss Brownlow wrote. The daughter of a professional woman, a midwife of all things. People were careful in those days in the making of suitable matches. What a coup! One that might only be achieved by someone in my aunt's position, I knew it. If only it had been that simple, though. It wasn't just a case of swanning in one day, parading past the rows of cots and crying babies as I'd imagined. I'd been earmarked.

Apart from these apparent offstage nudges, the path for the prospective adopters was far from straightforward. As I continued to journey through my early life story, revealed in stages by the file, tears flowed from my eyes.

Rose was appointed a guardian by the juvenile court, to keep a check on her progress in the care of her newfound foster parents. Miss Georgina Babbington-Thwaites, the person in question, gave heart-rending accounts of how Rose Keller had thrived in Mrs.Wetherby's care. Yes, lavish praise was heaped upon my mum, but not my dad. This upset me the most.

'I desire to adopt Rose Keller.'

The words rang in my ears. How could he not have been anything but a perfect father? Of the two of them he seemed to be the mover and shaker. I recalled Mum's words, uttered once during my adult years. A Mother's Day lunch, too much wine, too much talk, tongues loosening.

A tale of long ago, when Dad was away at sea. She'd joined her sister-in-law, later to become my Aunt Lorna, along with Uncle Henry, at a holiday cottage on the coast. Rest was needed, since she was three months pregnant. Uncle Henry was out sailing while Aunt Lorna prepared supper, hampered by my then one year old cousin Philip, who was constantly under her feet. Mum should take a walk along the promenade, she suggested, inhale fresh ozone, it did the world of good. And there was the pushchair; Philip loved to ride in it, loved to look out to sea at the sailing boats bobbing in the bay, point to 'Daddy'. They went there, the two of them, then they returned, and as Mum pushed my toddler cousin back uphill, globules of blood spattered the footpath.

'It was James who wanted children,' she said during the third glass of Liebfraumilch.

I didn't doubt it; taking on a child at forty-two wasn't something you went into lightly in those days. You didn't hire childcare to go out to work, continue in a well-thought-of profession. You stayed at home, slaved in the kitchen with little in the way of modern appliances – even if you had been entitled to more than most, from the NAAFI. You took the child on the bus to do the shopping, you bathed her, you fed her, you mopped the kitchen floor. It wasn't easy, especially when the child wasn't easy.

Hadn't she tried to be a mother, for God's sake? Several miscarriages. Even a doctor's decree that she must now lie flat on her back for the entire duration of a further pregnancy in order to give birth, assisted by Aunt Astrid's warnings of a possible Down's Syndrome child.

As to Commander Wetherby RN, he appeared not to like being interviewed, the missive said. Although co-operative, he clearly disliked the fact that his suitability with regard to future legalised fatherhood was being called into question. Of course he could supply references: there was an old naval crony he'd served with, a family man. What did they want to know exactly?

I'd found the letter Dad had written to Mum after that final miscarriage, when I was clearing out the attic after her death. Devastated he was, utterly so. The words carried an inexplicable gravitas that only now I fully understand.

10

Mr. McDonald

The indignity of being questioned as to paternal suitability! Especially after fighting for your country, suffering wartime ailments which take a later toll, refusing a medal much higher than the MBE because every sailor on board the aircraft carrier deserved one too. And because Dad never talked about the war, I wasn't aware of his wartime experience until soon after his untimely death, occurring a week before my eighteenth birthday.

I was staying with Aunt May, an elderly cousin of his. Along with her revelation about the medal came another.

'James's first wife always liked to go out on Friday nights,' she announced brightly one teatime. 'Whenever he was home from sea before the war, Rachel would be waiting for him in her dancing shoes.'

Stunned, I sat in silence while Aunt May, without pause, talked fondly of my dad. Musical evenings when cousins, aunts, uncles and friends gathered round a worn out upright, singing along. Aunt Lorna belting out Gilbert and Sullivan arias in her rich mezzo tones, while suitors with gold rings climbing up the arms of dark blue uniforms showered her with compliments.

A visit to pay respects at a war memorial, to find it draped with bodies while someone attempted a group photograph, all staring into the confined lens of an old box camera. They hadn't bargained on a pair of human antler horns appearing from behind them when later the photos were developed. Commander James Wetherby RN was no respecter of fools and always found a way to deflate deserving causes.

A schoolboy practical joker – yes. The attaching of string to opposite door knockers of terraced Portsmouth houses, hanging so that he could then ride a bicycle across them; cadging a lift to school on the back of a milk float until caught out. And marching up a garden path demanding to know the name of a piece of piano music he'd heard each day when coming home from school. Debussy's 'La fille aux cheveux de lin'. He'd taught himself from scratch, could play it well, I'd heard it many times, I told Aunt May. Crossing out 'de lin' in pencil and replacing with it with "d'or" – the girl with the golden hair.

Yes, Aunt May had a soft spot for my dad, tried desperately to model her only son Victor on him. Anyone less like Dad you couldn't hope to meet, Mum often said. Overweight, over-indulged and lazy. A sort of compliment in its way, a sort of wishful thinking.

But I'd never heard of a first wife, she'd never ever been mentioned. And although I was young for my age in some ways, I was sufficiently astute to conceal my lack of knowledge as to her existence. Aunt May was a kindly soul – she'd have been mortified, I knew it, setting a cat amongst the pigeons. But I wouldn't tell Mum. Did Mum even know? No – I wouldn't say anything, at least not yet.

She'd been a bit of a seamstress in her day – Aunt May – running up dresses for me when I was small. And, being the daughter of a much older sister of my dad's late mother, she took the place of a granny I never met.

'Terrible, that bomb was,' Aunt May continued, returning to the subject while boiling the electric kettle and making tea. 'The air raid warning had been sounded, Rachel tried to get James's mother out of bed and down to the shelter. But there wasn't time – suddenly the Heinkel was overhead, bomb doors opening. They took a direct hit. James's mother was blown right out of the window – the bed landed in the street with her inside it. Rachel was found in an understairs cupboard. Dead.'

Weak-kneed I sat down at the tiny kitchen table, watching the steam rise from the kettle, unable to speak. Aunt May seemed not to have noticed, as if she'd gone back in time and forgotten I was there.

'With James away in the Med, Henry sent a telegram from the Admiralty – Lorna told me. Somehow James never got it, came home one day armed with little gifts, but the house was all gone, nothing left – just an empty hole amongst the row of terraces.'

The news shook me to the core, and brought back

other revelations that had exploded onto my already shattered childhood landscape, resulting in profound perplexity in the mind of a seven-year-old child. It was about a year after my parents had told me I was adopted.

It hadn't been unusual for Dad to disappear off for a few days from time to time, going on business trips around the country. So I thought nothing of it when he was away for a while, even though it was a bit longer than on other occasions.

I was then just a trifle baffled when Mum drove to the local hospital, where she'd gone back to work part time in physiotherapy. After she parked our old dark green Morris Eight on the main road outside St. Jude's, she reached over into the back seat and removed a brown paper bag. 'Sharp Eyes', as I was called, spotted the contents, a pair of Dad's blue and white striped pyjamas. I wanted to know why she was taking them into the hospital with her.

'A poor man needs them,' she replied quickly.

'What's the man's name?' I demanded.

'Mr. McDonald.'

Mum locked the car door and marched across the main road with the paper bag in hand while I waited alone in the car. I couldn't help but feel sorry for poor Mr. McDonald, who appeared not to have enough pyjamas of his own. Perhaps, as a part-time physiotherapist, Mum took pity on such creatures, helped them where she could. And since Dad was away on business, he wasn't exactly going to miss them, was he?

Then Aunt Astrid came to stay. Reluctantly, I realise, Mum needed help looking after me. Dad was in hospital, in St. Jude's. That explained the pyjamas. It also explained – to some degree at least – Mr. McDonald. There was no such person requiring Mum's charity, the change of pyjamas had been for Dad.

But why invent Mr. McDonald? Why not tell the truth? I was going to find out sooner or later, my seven year old brain figured. Why not do so straightaway? Explanations were needed after all, how Dad was going to have to have a lot of rest; there was no way I'd be allowed to gleefully leap onto the bed like I used to do on weekend mornings. Yes, things seemed pretty serious. I didn't get it, and just then I began not to trust grown-ups anymore. It was a role I assumed with certain ability, laid down long before.

Another trip to St. Jude's before Dad was released. Another pair of pyjamas in another brown paper bag. This time we were accompanied by Aunt Astrid. She and I waited for Mum in the car.

'Why didn't you ever marry?' I piped up from the back seat.

Her voice was crisp, matter of fact.

'Because I wasn't lucky enough to meet someone like your daddy – that's why.'

Veering off this topic, she announced:

'You might have had another aunt you know, Julie. Beautiful she was, with pale golden hair. Just like Granny Tanner when she was a young girl.'

A further sister, younger than Mum, called Emily. I listened, enthralled. What had happened to her? I demanded to know. She and Mum caught diphtheria, were put in a hospital isolation ward, that's what happened.

Quite a bit older, and a medical student back then, Aunt Astrid described how she'd stood beside her parents, Granny and Grandpa Tanner, staring at the younger sisters through a glass panel, giving advice. I could imagine Aunt Astrid doing that with considerable ease, until there was no need for it anymore. From the morning when Mum woke to find her little sister ashen faced and still in the bed beside her. Granny Tanner never allowed Emily's name to be mentioned again. The subject was taboo.

It was only natural then, a few days after Dad was out of hospital, convalescing in bed, and Aunt Astrid had returned home, for me to tell Mum what I'd learned. Just like Dad, when years later I announced how Aunt Astrid claimed she'd paid for their engagement dinner, I'd never seen Mum so cross.

'Trust Dr. Astrid Tanner!' she fumed.

Mum always called her elder sister by her full title when she didn't approved of something she'd gone and done. Like the time Aunt Astrid found us Peeko, a seal point Siamese kitten.

11

The Sibling

Peeko arrived in a wicker basket, piercing deep-blue eyes set within a chocolate-brown, furry face staring out at us in fear. I'd never seen a kitten – or indeed a cat – like him; he was a special breed from a place called Siam. Had my dad collected him from there? I wanted to know. This was met with certain amusement. No! Peeko came from London.

Someone Aunt Astrid knew bred Siamese, I learned. Peeko, as the runt of the litter, was the last to find a home. It marked him out as unwanted and special. Hence a kind of love-hate relationship between the two of us came about, which laid down my lifelong affection for cats and devotion to cat ownership. I identified with him.

That Aunt Astrid had masterminded the whole thing was a matter about which I sensed Mum and Dad were not entirely happy, as though she'd meddled in their lives once more. But the poor woman, for all her self-imposed 'head of the family' nonsense, was most likely genuine in her desire to fulfil a need that had been lacking within our own small unit. She desired recognition and thanks of course, and when she received neither, reminded everyone of what she'd done for them. Peeko was no exception.

His arrival therefore took place some weeks before the matter of my adoption was raised around the oak drop-leaf table. All because of my desire for a sibling. My school friends had brothers and sisters and I wanted to have one too. In fact, I'd thought my plan quite ingenious and couldn't wait to break it to my parents.

From the back seat of the old green Morris Eight, I told Mum of my bright idea as she was driving to pick up Dad from work. They should have another baby – what could be easier? By the time Dad climbed into the passenger seat beside her, I was in full flow, and I repeated my suggestion – no, request! – to them both. I can still see the exchange of looks, and even at my tender age comprehended that I'd infringed on something difficult.

Despite the need to travel to London by train and bring back Peeko in a crowded railway carriage – doubtless evoking memories of another trip to London, to fetch me – Dad was clearly a cat lover. He adored Peeko, and Peeko, not unsurprisingly, became his cat. But the kitten's arrival was an affair of mixed feelings to begin with, not least for myself.

I so wanted a playmate, but however much I tried to engage Peeko in games with me, he refused. He would run away and hide, as being pestered by a little girl was not a pleasant experience. Then I had another bright idea – siblings wore clothes. Perhaps if I dressed Peeko up he'd feel better disposed towards me? So I rummaged in a drawer and produced an old vest, one of Eva's hand-me-downs via Aunt Verity, by that time too small for me. A perfect fit!

While Mum was outside on the front lawn, bent over a flower bed, weeding, I forced one front leg then the other through each sleeve hole, against wild feline protestation. Peeko lashed out and caught the side of my face with needle-like talons, narrowly missing my eye. I screamed. Mum dropped her trowel and ran into the lounge through the open French window.

'Julie – you stupid girl!' she shouted. 'Whatever are you doing? – the animal could have had your eye out!'

Peeko ran off, clothed in the vest, and hid behind a bookcase. And I ran off too, out through the French windows like a bat out of hell, ran and ran until I reached the narrow lane between the back gardens of neighbouring houses, where I sat down to rest and catch my breath.

At that moment I really did want to run away for good. I was angry and the anger was spreading from somewhere deep inside. But where to go I'd no idea. So I sat there amongst tall grasses beneath a high privet hedge, hot tears mixed with fresh red blood pouring down my cheek onto one of Aunt May's summer dresses.

An angry dog issued a menacing bark from a nearby garden; my heart pounded.

'Titus!' a man's raucous voice yelled.

I'd seen the huge, dark-coated German shepherd dog walked on a lead by his owner, a big, burly, cross-tempered man. I was always glad we were in the car when the pair of them passed by. I was scared of Titus – and the man. I'd have to return home.

My feet thundered along the path away from Titus's barks and the man's shouting. Soon I reached the side gate which led into the apple orchard, and hid behind our garden shed. I could hear Mum calling me in the distance from the road, her voice desperate:

'Julie! Julie! – where are you? – please come back!'

There were other ways to play with Peeko, Mum advised in a kindlier tone some days later. An old envelope folded into pleats, with a long piece of string tied round it so the two halves fanned out like a butterfly's wings. I could trail it behind me, Peeko would follow – just try it, she urged. To my delight, it worked, and I marched round the house with the envelope following in my wake. It was like dragging a dying bird, or a mouse. Peeko leapt out from nowhere, jumped onto the envelope, and scuffled it with his sharp claws. Just when he thought he'd caught it, and began to tear it to pieces, I moved on, and the frustrated kitten scampered behind me. I took a perverse sort of pleasure in this activity: *'You wouldn't play with me properly and this is how I'm going to repay you!'*

I hated it when Peeko chose to go on Dad's lap in preference to my own when I grew older. We'd kind of made things up, in a way, the memory of the tantrumous little girl not quite forgotten, just as my bid to run away was not forgotten by my parents.

Soon after being told I was adopted, my bedroom door began to be locked at night and a chamber pot placed on the floor. It was for my own safety, Mum said, there'd been some break-ins in the area. It was true; Dad had recently caught some boys stealing apples, picked from the orchard, which were stored in our outhouse. They'd managed to get in through a downstairs toilet window, so I was scared.

I stayed awake at night, imagining a burglar climbing onto the roof then entering my bedroom. Or Titus, breaking free and racing into the garden, lying in wait until the following day. Yes, the door was better locked.

One weekend, soon after my attempt to run away, we went to stay with Aunt Lorna and Uncle Henry. Peeko was put in the cattery, and later, when we returned home, we discovered that he'd pined for us throughout our time away, and had hardly eaten a thing. Everyone felt guilty, even me. He loved us, after all.

Uncle Henry, unlike Dad, was still a serving officer in the Royal Navy, and my parents had been invited to attend a ball with them at the Royal Naval Barracks in Portsmouth. On the day of the ball, I was despatched with Alice, cousin Philip's younger sister, to the tree-house at the bottom of my aunt and uncle's garden, along with a picnic tea: bread rolls with homemade blackcurrant jam, slabs of fruit cake and orange squash. Dad, Uncle Henry and Philip went sailing and Mum and Aunt Lorna took it in turns to go the hair-dressers while the other stayed behind to keep an eye on us. Once the hairdos were complete, a blonde chignon for Aunt Lorna and the usual black, rolled-up into the base of the neck style for Mum, we were given strict instructions not to disturb them.

Evening dresses, still under wraps, were hung over the tops of wardrobe doors, Alice explained. Next, cucumber slices, used as beauty treatments, were placed over the eyes, while our mothers rested up on their respective beds. Alice was used to these occasions when her parents got dressed up. I so wanted a sister who could share such secrets with me all the time, wished Alice could be one. But she was my cousin and I dared not tell her she wasn't even my 'real' one anymore, in case she wanted nothing more to do with me.

A neighbour arrived to childmind, and the three of us were packed off to bed after a high tea in the kitchen. We shared a room, Alice and I, twin beds side by side, much to her chagrin I suspect, as she was three years older than me.

‘I wish we could see them leave for the ball,’ I said.

‘Of course we can – stupid! We’ll stand on tiptoe and watch them through the landing window – no-one will hear us.’

‘But we’ll be locked in!’ I objected.

Alice peered down her nose at me.

‘Of course we won’t – whatever gave you that idea?’

12

Bathed in a Different Light

As I leafed through the file, my adoption narrative continued. I'd e-mailed Angela the same day she'd passed it on to me, having read the whole thing through from cover to cover. A story one couldn't put down.

'It does make sense,' I said, knowing at one level that it did, in purely chronological, factual terms. I was, in the desire to get from the beginning to the end as fast as possible, attempting to quench my insistent appetite for knowledge. I was desperate to understand something awful, a kind of shock reaction along with the presenting of a brave face to the adoption society, my body clothed in valiant armour. I had a reputation to sustain: a person of mature and sound mind, as considered in cold legalistic terms by the judge.

Certainly the file explained some things, a series of bureaucratic missives that sealed the matter for good, so that it could be laid to rest in a dust-gathering vault. But how long might these undisturbed pieces of personal history remain there? I couldn't help but wonder back then. Beyond the lives of those who were the subject matter? And would the original of the file in front of me eventually be destroyed along with all the others?

Perhaps I, myself, might decide to get rid of my own copy one day, have it burned, before someone, in an official capacity, could lay their hands on it, and do it for me after my death? Except for that one handwritten letter.

'I desire to adopt Rose Keller.'

I would bury it – incinerated – with me.

So there the file lay, on the oak drop-leaf table, skimmed over, to be returned to as the implications of the tale began to sink in. Each time I re-read it, dwelt on its contents, the stage curtain drew open to reveal another scene, bathed in different lighting, darker contours. Constant checks made on Rose Keller, medical tests to see if the baby, temporarily entrusted to the Wetherbys' care, was healthy.

What if Rose Keller hadn't been healthy? Would the law court have deemed her unsuitable for adoption? Would she have been considered too big a responsibility for a middle-aged couple? Indeed – would the Wetherbys have wanted to keep her? Surely so, a bond was forming. But would they have been allowed to do so? And if not, where would Rose Keller have ended up?

Tests passed with flying colours, adoption seemed set to take place. Even my dad was deemed fit, after a further interview with his wartime naval colleague had been carried out by the authorities. Yes – Commander Wetherby would make an excellent father, he'd said.

But there was another hoop to jump through. Agreement by the birth parents to give up all rights to their daughter. This was when things didn't go entirely to plan, not for my apprehensive foster parents, but for Joyce.

Like the 1940 air raid, the imagined scene has played itself over and over. Joyce's return home one day to be greeted by stoney-faced parents. The three of them gathered in the front lounge of the bay-windowed, detached mock-Tudor house, the one I'd located on Google Maps. It was situated at the address Joyce had been requested to provide for necessary inclusion on my original birth certificate.

Visible through the bay window, a neat lawn presented an array of fragrant rose blooms in a central bed: red, white, yellow, peachy-pink, lovingly tended by Joyce's mum, herself a Rose. Baby Rose had been named after her, yet never met her. Now, the grandmother simply knew that Rose as a name in the typewritten letter which she held in her hands. It had arrived open, Joyce said, they'd looked inside.

Of course they would – they needed something tangible on which to hang suspicions. What better than a stout manilla envelope, bearing a postmark from somewhere far away from Joyce's home? Why hadn't their daughter arranged to have it sent to the nursing home, where she had recently secured a new job? Was she frightened that someone in authority might find it, question her? And was she frightened of getting the sack for an offence of which she was clearly guilty? No wonder Joyce had been so anxious to come home on her off-duty weekend, she must have been expecting the piece of correspondence.

Joyce had lied, Rose and Robert Keller were convinced of it. Why fling in a sought-after hospital job? It was something that Joyce, despite their doubts, had wanted to do since childhood – become a nurse. Heart set on it, she'd signed up without their consent on leaving school, at sixteen. Now she was a midwife, claimed to love her job.

Never a very maternal person, their daughter. How they wished otherwise, wished she could have married that Charles Dempsey fellow. Practical and determined, she was. Hot tempered too, so much so that her German grandmother had once locked her in the cellar for being rebellious. Joyce hated her grandmother, but, although she would never admit it, she was like her. Headstrong, bossy, passionate.

Joyce had spun a plausible yarn, said she'd seen a nursing home advertised in a professional magazine, far away in the south east of England. What could be better, a change of scene, a new opportunity? But why would she want to move away so far from the boyfriend who still refused to leave her alone since she'd returned to the area?

Her letters home had been few, until she wrote to

say the job hadn't lived up to her expectations. All of a sudden she had another, nearer home again, in another nursing home. But it was no longer the job she'd yearned for in the big general hospital, one that she'd thrown up, out of the blue, months before.

Why hadn't she owned up – explained her absence away from the area? Why hide the birth of their granddaughter? Did she really think they were so mean that they wouldn't have tried to help her – help the child? That was the worst part. And now the adoption wheels were set in motion, foster parents were ready to take on their only grandchild, the one they'd always hoped for.

Joyce was so sure she and Charles had covered every contingency, she continued. They weren't even going to sign the agreement from anywhere nearby for fear of a horrid little rumour leaking out. Hush-hush, it had to be. And Rose's guardian, Miss Georgina Babbington-Thwaites, was working on behalf of a juvenile court. Rose was far away, in Portsmouth, where her adoption would take place – that is, if she, Joyce, and the putative father, were in agreement.

It was all set up, she told her parents, things had gone too far to be reversed now. Charles Dempsey wouldn't marry her, his mother hated her, hated anyone who threatened to take her only son away. She'd claimed to be an invalid; it was an excuse, Joyce was sure of it. And the woman had threatened to write her son out of her will if he went against her wishes.

* * *

The pair had indeed arranged to sign the adoption consent forms, which had been enclosed with the letter, at an office in a town fifty miles away. But with their cover blown, the presiding official was greeted by a much distressed Joyce, blaming the authorities for messing things up. Why hadn't Rose's guardian been more careful?

Regardless, it had to be done: did they both still wish to go through with it? Were they sure they both wanted to give up their child for adoption? Charles readily agreed, the file recorded; Joyce was angry and upset.

The signed forms were returned to Miss Babbington-Thwaites, along with a letter in Joyce's handwriting, now lying there in the file, contained amongst the other evidence. This carelessness had caused *'great inconvenience',* she accused. The letter had left the office firmly sealed, Miss Babbington-Thwaites retaliated.

And so the date for the adoption was set, involving more correspondence, this time exchanged between Margery Brownlow and the guardian. Miss Brownlow planned to attend the court hearing and vouch for Rose's likeness, even though she hadn't seen her for four months and babies can change a lot in that time. What if the baby hadn't been Rose – would Miss Brownlow have known?

The week before the court hearing, my parents arranged to have me christened in the local parish church. I'd kept the certificate, never before realising the date's significance. Looking at it again I saw that they hadn't waited until I was, in the eyes of the law, officially theirs. But in the eyes of the church Rose Keller no longer existed and Julie Wetherby did. Mum always said a child should be christened as soon as possible. Just in case. Had she been thinking of baby Rose's early sickness? And had she been thinking of her younger sister Emily, lost to her in childhood?

Days later, on that tacky piece of paper called a birth certificate, issued by the authorities, the legally endorsed Julie Wetherby came into being. As did the embryo of her younger sister, Brenda Keller.

13

The Season of Goodwill

2009 wore on, and when Christmas began to appear in the shops, I'd almost given up on ever finding Joyce. With Diane reluctantly at the helm, the social services department seemed to be taking their time. Joyce, if really alive, was eighty-seven, for goodness sake!

Then a letter arrived at the offices of the adoption society. It contained apologies for the delay, and a request for more information. In order to go into the database, Diane and her team required copies of Joyce's birth and marriage certificates. Again, I contacted the Government Registry Office and, again, forked out.

The copies arrived, once more by express delivery, and were immediately dispatched to Angela. A further wait ensued. Eventually communication with my adoption counsellor was made, and from there on things seemed to accelerate with such speed I could barely get my head round it. What had until then been a story on paper was fast becoming a reality.

There were still potential further hold ups, since Diane was now questioning whether or not Joyce had, at some stage, signed a declaration with a national adoption register requesting anonymity. But if that path was to be pursued out of dogged persistence in doing things by the rule book – their rule book – Diane might find herself having to face the fact that an old lady had expired within the period of further procrastination. Angela, I suspect, conveyed to her my innermost fears.

Beginning to become clear though, while not explicitly saying so, was that they'd found her. The next thing I knew, Diane had a visit to Joyce marked in her diary. Was I hearing correctly? Before I could properly absorb this, Angela called me one afternoon. Christmas was but one week away and Diane had been to see Joyce.

I decided to write Joyce a letter. By this time I badly wanted to meet her, since it had also occurred to me that she might be in a home, or at the very least, in sheltered housing. This could be our last chance. Despite all the stuff I'd picked up in the file, there was no reason to suppose that Joyce hadn't spent every day of every passing year regretting her actions, wondering what had happened to me and wondering if she had made the right decision.

I wanted to show her that she had. That, in spite of the temper tantrums, cover-ups and other consequences of being an adopted child, I'd grown up in a happy home with parents I'd adored, and, in many ways, had made a successful job of life. Besides, it was the season of goodwill.

* * *

I'd selected a photo of myself, taken at friends' on my 60th birthday. My plan had been for it to be posted to Joyce with the letter. However, in conference with Angela, I decided to first send a photocopy along with a copy of the letter, for Diane to peruse. It turned out to be a good move in several ways. Written from the heart and sent via the adoption society, like all correspondence in the early stages, the letter was a tear-jerker. A softer side of Diane was coming to the fore.

How could the letter *not* have moved someone, though? With the celebration of nativity just days away, the reappearance of a daughter after sixty years, desiring to say 'hello' to her mother, could hardly be cast aside. By this time I was excited and clutching at straws, imagining that I might need to be escorted by Diane to wherever Joyce was living, introduced to a care home owner or a warden, then be permitted a few moments of time with her, alone.

'Rose!' she'd murmur, 'I thought this moment would never come!'

Small, frail and chair-bound, tears of regret and guilt would fill her eyes. I'd enfold her in my arms. We'd hug, hold each other tight, talk a little, until our time was up and Diane needed to lead me away. To achieve that, to look upon the face of my birth mother, was something that I'd never in my wildest dreams imagined possible. This was beginning to feel like the best Christmas for a very long time.

And that's all I was asking for. To say 'hello.' So, in

order not to put Joyce off, I assured her that no-one need know about the matter. And why should they? This would be, if only it could be pulled off, our private moment together. Our only moment.

Diane then talked with Joyce, told her about the copy of the photograph.

'May I see it?' Joyce responded.

Diane removed it from her bag and placed it in Joyce's hands. She stared at it for a very long time.

Angela assisted me with the writing of my letter. I included a bit of background about myself, how I'd grown up in a happy home with my adoptive parents, that I'd led a successful professional life. And as it was Christmas, I'd wanted to acknowledge that in some way. Not a card, that was way too over the top just then, but a rather splendid little sticker I'd managed to find in an arty stationary shop. Two little birds, side by side on a branch. I'd bought a spare, as a precaution, since I guessed that in my anxiety to get it all right I might spoil the first attempt through nerves.

'Take your time,' Angela soothed as I signed my name with trembling hand, 'we can make further copies if need be.'

And so the typewritten letter was posted, along with a copy of the same photograph – one Joyce could keep, this time. Also enclosed was a covering note from Angela explaining the intermediary role she was playing, and the adoption society's hours of opening in the New Year. Interestingly, and hearteningly, Joyce had requested that Diane and her department no longer play a part in the matter, preferring instead to deal directly with Angela, in turn bringing herself a step closer to me.

All over the Christmas period, which I spent partially alone and partially with friends, I could think of little else. In the evenings, in my apartment, I sat in magical awe with all lights turned off, save the ones that winked from the Christmas tree, as seasonal messages and carols on the radio wafted over me.

In my mind I saw the manger scene, Mary and Joseph and the infant Jesus in swaddling clothes, hidden away. And I saw the golden-haired infant, enveloped in a blanket, laid within a wicker basket, thrashing out her limbs in despair as her future was discussed. Not born in a stable, but down some long corridor, I imagined, at the back of the nursing home, out of sight. Raised eyebrows, exchanged whisperings:

'The mother's a midwife – should have known better.' 'The disgrace of it all, and now she's planning to leave her child behind while she goes back to work!' 'Maybe – just maybe – there's a solution. A childless couple – the mother's a physiotherapist. The perfect match!'

Could we cross that divide, Joyce and I, even for a few sweet moments, basking in seasonal optimism? No gifts from wise men paying homage, but the gift of a child to a mother, returned after years of separation. One that, to grandparents, had remained but a name on a sheet of paper: Rose Keller junior, destined to be signed away.

And to that child, the gift of a mother – another one – who'd once held her in her arms, restored at last. It was something special, beyond price, not wrapped in Christmas paper beneath a decorated tree, but something that was meant to be, was always meant to be, I felt sure of it. Inspired by a voice in my head at the beginning of the year:

'You must start your search.'

14

Getting Down to Basics

'I knew this was going to happen.'

Joyce's words to my counsellor, uttered down the phone at 9.00am precisely on the morning of January 4th, 2010, just as the adoption society opened its doors for business after the holiday. How did she know? I wondered. How was she so apparently imbued with such a sense of purpose, enabling her to forge ahead without wasting a minute, thinking of little else since Diane's visit?

'Please thank Julie for giving me a second chance,' she'd added.

On hearing this my chest exploded in a cocktail of joy and sadness; joy at the hope of something deep and meaningful as to the future of the relationship, sadness at the wasted years that lay between us.

'What happens now?' I asked.

'Some housekeeping,' Angela replied.

Housekeeping? What did that mean?

'Joyce needs to make sure that other parties are in agreement,' my counsellor explained. 'It's what always has to happen when initial contact with the birth family is made.'

'To ensure the coast is clear?' I queried.

'Indeed. But things are looking hopeful, Julie. Joyce's partner has been behind her in this; he's positively encouraging her to go ahead.'

So what was standing in the way? My sister? Yes, she was a full one; Joyce had said so. We were both daughters of Charles Walton Dempsey after all, a matter about which I still had mixed feelings.

I'd performed a Google search to see if anyone by the name of Brenda Fernández could be traced to an area, to an address even. Unlike my other investigations, I'd drawn a complete blank. I'd hoped perhaps that she was out of the country, out of the way. And what was this about a partner? Was Joyce, after all these years, living in sin – as seen by members of her generation – in a gesture of defiance?

'Will that block matters?'

'It depends, Julie. We're in the early stages still, these things can take time. But in the meantime, Joyce has replied to your letter – I'm forwarding it to you. She's enclosed some photographs of herself.'

Photographs! My heart skipped a beat. Soon, very soon, I'd see someone close to me, my own kith and kin, not just distant stares projected upon me from rows of glazed eyes facing a camera lens, in full Edwardian family pose. My mind roved back along the path I'd travelled to this point, and I tried to put myself in Joyce's shoes. This wasn't the person I'd envisaged at all, an old lady, frail and at the end of her life, holding on to a few stray threads in the hope of redemption. And she wasn't like the mother who'd fallen from a wheelchair and collapsed onto the linoleum floor of a geriatric hospital ward just as her daughter had phoned to enquire about her. Instead, she was someone, who, at the very same age, possessed not only her faculties, but – yes! – a partner. Robust, as Diane had described her, which, in turn, had given me a certain amount of self-satisfied pleasure. The social worker's attempts at protecting an old woman from the shock of being faced with a past she thought she'd long since buried, had been proven far from necessary. But with this knowledge came new implications, new fantasies, ones that I hoped wouldn't be dashed by the non-cooperation of a family member.

'Did Joyce wonder how we tracked her down?' I enquired.

'Diane told her that information is available for all to see these days – online. Joyce said she'd been given to understand that this was so.'

I tried to ignore the twist of warning in the pit of my stomach.

'Life: Part Two' was taking a further abrupt turn. The third instalment. Since I'd got involved in the time-consuming ancestry investigations, I'd begun to access parts of me I'd never been consciously aware of before. Sensations going beyond any recognisable, tangible feelings were exposed, as though buried down a dank, dark well. Soft, spongy and peculiar, they had lain there since before time. And now something even more elemental was being touched upon.

Joyce's handwriting, discernibly the same style as in the copy of that letter to Miss Georgina Babbington-Thwaites of sixty years ago, which still lay amongst the other documentation in my file. The anger it provoked! – brought forth from deep inside me each time I'd re-read it. The imperious tone, lashing out at those who deserved no blame. There was no mistaking the same hand, no forgetting the *'great inconvenience'* at Miss Georgina Babbington-Thwaites's suggested carelessness over the apparently unsealed letter. How it had wrecked matters, brought to the attention of Joyce's parents a grandchild they'd never known about, never needed to have known about. Hidden, secret, the cleverly concocted plan torn to smithereens.

'Hello,' the letter to me began. The pen had seemingly scurried across the page, words tumbling over one another. They presented a brief history of Joyce: sporting interests when growing up and continuing through life. Hockey, tennis; later, golf. Dog ownership – no cats were mentioned. Gardening, tending roses in particular, just as her own mother had done. And baking. Nursing – yes, how she'd disobeyed her parents' wishes, she crowed. What had they wanted of her? I wondered. Some low-key job, marking time before becoming first a wife, then a mother? And there was no mention of music, writing, or painting. We didn't seem

to have much in common at all.

She spoke of a boy she'd gone out with for seven years, as if he was nothing at all to do with me. At least that dissolved the tacky thoughts of a one night stand in some fifth-rate hotel bedroom. Charles Dempsey, as I'd discovered via the ancestry site, had been some kind of agent, listed up until the early seventies in an old phonebook, living at the same address he'd been at when signing the form of consent.

Joyce also alluded to her decision to *'get me adopted'*, as she put it, especially as she hadn't wanted to upset *'Mum'* and *'Dad.'* Already I wanted to scream. What was there about me that could upset anyone? Because, no matter what rationalisations anyone might offer me, it didn't sit well at all.

At the end:

'Best Wishes,

Joyce.'

The spirit of Christmas was fast evaporating. While on the one hand I was excited to have heard from Joyce, and the response was a positive one – especially in the light of cousin Eva's experiences – I felt short-changed. But there was more. Inside the letter, contained within a folded piece of blank paper, were the photographs.

Several were in colour, one of Joyce in her early fifties, according to the date written in blue pen on the back, taken with a black Labrador. She was seated on the floor, leaning against the foot of an armchair, the dog beside her. She stared off to the side, as though detached, haunted by things she kept locked away and wouldn't look at in the eye. This wasn't a happy lady.

Another showed her about twenty years later, taken outside, walking in the countryside, dressed in tartan trousers, green wellies and a navy Guernsey sweater. Although she smiled at the camera there was still that look, the suggestion of a burden buried deep within, as though she herself, unaided, held down the lid with firm hands.

And the last, I'd tried to ignore it until then. Not look. Black and white, head and shoulders. And now I held it in my hands, as Joyce had held the picture of me taken on my sixtieth birthday. A young woman's face, scintillating with joy, head tilted just so slightly, eyes sideways at the corners, surely smiling at a man. There was no mistaking that expression.

In that moment I knew her, recognised her face, associated it with something so immensely painful my body erupted. I didn't care that the people in adjacent apartments could hear me, might think I'd taken leave of my senses. I was a child in a cot, contained within the four walls of a nursing home, abandoned. I screamed and screamed.

I screamed because there was an aspect of me in that face, not immediately discernible, but there all the same. I screamed because she looked so happy. And I screamed because a man had taken precedence over her baby, once more. The evidence was written on the back, again in blue pen.

'The first photo Desmond took of me.

September 1950.'

It was just two months after Brenda Keller was born.

15

Little Girl Lost

She wanted to be there, waiting on the beach, towel in hand. She longed to enfold her child as she emerged from the light greenish-blue water that foamed on the yellow sand. The little girl in the pale blue swimsuit and white floppy sunhat, windswept fringe of gold peeking through. Tears rolled down the mother's cheeks, heart bursting with regret and self-admonishment.

Joyce's confession, made to Angela, after yet another photograph from the album of my past, this time in faded colour, landed in an envelope on her doormat. Our exchange of letters via the adoption society had continued, as each revealed to the other small things about our lives, always careful not to say too much. A new Joyce was beginning to emerge. One who desired even closer access to her child.

Angela seemed to have won her trust, apparently giving Joyce a chance to express things that, for years, had been repressed. And there was another ray of hope – it lay with her partner, who I'd assumed would be a widower she'd met socially. This man appeared to be behind her reconnection with me – had given her every encouragement to go ahead – my counsellor told me.

Already my heart warmed to him.

'The girl must come and stay!' he'd pronounced.

In spite of the fact that nothing concrete concerning the subject of Brenda had yet come to the fore, I liked this idea; it bore the marks of acceptance and inclusivity. But how could I go there, to that four-bedroom house on a cliff near the sea, as Joyce had described it to Angela? How could I stay under their roof, just me alone with them? I wasn't yet ready for that. I'd have to think of an alternative arrangement that wouldn't in the first instance offend, since a future meeting now seemed a certainty.

Joyce was still an enigma to me though, and I didn't like to push too hard. Neither, I suspect, did Angela. Everything had to be handled with the utmost care and diplomacy – one wrong move would possibly destroy everything we'd achieved so far.

Was the coast really clear? I asked. Angela understood my concerns and explained that had Joyce not lived at the opposite end of the country, she would by now have paid her a visit herself, found out how she and the partner were placed. With Diane and the local adoption team out of the equation, we had to trust – both of us – that the positive signals being emitted were evidence enough that all was well.

'Joyce has been used to hiding things for most of her life; she's a very defended lady,' my counsellor warned. 'Revealing family matters won't be second nature to her. But she mentioned Brenda to me, so she has admitted to the fact that she has not just one daughter, but two.'

I didn't know how to react to this, a sister about whom I knew little, except for the discovery that she was, after all, resident in the UK. I'd so craved a sibling when young, yet I'd grown up as an only child. So had she. My sudden appearance on the scene might be too much to stomach, and the fact that she hadn't been mentioned suggested she could be lying low, unhappy about my appearance. I was, after all, the elder daughter.

Would she resent me as I had resented her? I had better reason, I told myself: discarded as a baby, while she was kept. It was as if she'd been a replacement, a consolation prize to appease wounded grandparents.

Could Julie telephone her? Joyce asked Angela, some weeks into the continued exchange of letters and enclosures via the adoption society. When presented with this suggestion, I hesitated, tongue-tied. What would I say to her? What could we possibly have to chat about?

'Just take your time,' Angela reassured me. 'There's no hurry, none at all; in fact, you don't *have* to talk until you meet in person.'

I knew, though, that it would be better for me to talk to Joyce beforehand. And so a date and time was fixed to telephone.

It was a Sunday. All day I dreaded it. My heart fluttered and my stomach swirled as I counted down the hours. For a full five minutes beforehand I circled the area by the wall-mounted phone, looking at my watch as the minutes ticked away. I placed my hand on the receiver, eyes still on the timepiece, until the moment arrived. Then I lifted the receiver and punched in the number.

For a matter of seconds it rang. A gap, a palpable silence – then a voice. Headmistress-ish. Imperious – the voice of the letter to Miss Babbington-Thwaites. Yet pleasant, and also vulnerable, in its way.

'Hello.'

The word I'd wanted to say, she'd said first.

'It's Julie.'

Another tangible silence, while the sound of my voice apparently sank in.

'I think you're being very brave,' she said at last.

What did that mean? Of course I knew I was, knew what every adoptee knows when they set out on their search. That at any point in the process they risk a rebuff, like cousin Eva, or that they may stray into uncharted territory where possible motives are brought into focus, even if not articulated. They know that they have put themselves into a kind of danger, exposed to people who have been around each other for years, a stranger amongst the familiar. They know that they subject themselves to a roller-coaster of emotion, as I'd already experienced, and they know that however hard they try, there will be nothing that can change the reality of a lifetime of separation. Was this a warning of some kind? Or simply a recognition of a big step I'd taken, that many might decide against? Or both?

And here we were, at either end of a telephone line. Intimate strangers.

'I know,' I replied.

What happened after that is a blur, some sort of chit-chat that continued for forty minutes. Mention of politics at odds with Brenda's own at one point, her name aired idly without elucidation. They were always arguing, Joyce said, as though that might make things better, laughing it off. Garden designs, rose cultivation; these subjects rolled off her tongue. I paused to consider the irony. Then she was onto trips abroad and barbecues. Golf tournaments were thrown in as well. I 'yes-ed' and 'no-ed' in the right places – at least I thought I had. Each of us on our best, politest behaviour, socially adept.

I thought of the child in the sea with the sunbonnet, and the tears shed by a mother. They belonged to a different woman to the one with whom I'd spoken, and with whom I continued to speak periodically over the next weeks. I so desired to access this other person, hidden away. Then I thought of the portrait – of course! – it was the answer.

Me when I was two years of age, wearing one of

Aunt May's dresses, sewn by hand, in bright emerald cotton printed with small white dots. The child, and the dress, were visible from the waist up. Behind the subject, a coastal seascape near where I spent my early years. I have a vague recollection of Mum and Dad taking me inside a dark studio and my photo being taken, since undertaking a real sitting at that age wouldn't have been possible. The artist achieved a good likeness, and for years it graced the sitting room walls, until, after Dad died and we moved to another area, it was relocated to the attic because it embarrassed me. The equivalent of uncool. There it had stayed ever since, even after Mum's passing. Eventually I'd cleared out the house before it was sold, and took the portrait away with me, next placing it at the back of a walk-in cupboard in my apartment, encased in bubble wrap. Forgotten.

Now I exposed it to the light of day, stared at the pensive child with the pale gold, wavy hair in the green dress, and felt both guilt and regret at having hidden her away for all those years. As Joyce had been so moved by the faded colour photo of me in the sea, she was bound to like the portrait. The more I thought about it, the more obvious it was. A gesture, a chance to give her back something she had lost: her child.

I also decided to make her an album of my life. Selecting photographs from different stages, I had copious copies made, and bought a smart leather album. It was an expensive enterprise which took many hours to produce. By now I was convinced that this was a way of melding the elements of my past, of finding the means to deal with the relinquishment and snuffing out of Rose Keller and the emergence of Julie Wetherby. Perhaps it would help Joyce to do so too? Or perhaps it was just something I alone needed to engage in? A kind of therapy, a making sense of things and a celebration of my life, when lately it had seemed so confused – battered, broken and betrayed.

Thus the album and the portrait were bundled up, addressed to Joyce and taken to the post office. We had direct communication now, direct connection.

16

The Past Revisited

The railway carriage packed, Rose lay in Joyce's arms, wrapped in a blanket on loan from the nursing home. By the end of the day, the mother would have to return it, empty. She hadn't seen her child for three whole weeks, and Rose sensed it. The infant wriggled, thrashing out soft pale limbs in rebellion, announcing to all that she mistrusted this person, disliked being placed near the maternal bosom that yielded no milk. Accusing eyes rose above the tops of newspapers, others frowned, then looked away out of the window. Even the small brass curtain ring, placed on the fourth finger of Joyce's left hand, failed to save the situation. Rose had marked her out, the woman who'd abandoned her.

When they reached the London terminus, Joyce gathered her child up as fellow travellers gathered up bags and briefcases. Once onto the station forecourt she instructed a taxi driver to take her to an address in Baker Street, where she and Rose would be parted forever. Rose would be placed in the arms of Margery Brownlow, who, in turn, would place her in the arms of another. She mustn't think about that – she mustn't!

It was as I'd reconstructed it, from information in the file and from things that Joyce had told my counsellor. And from things in my imagination. The train journey of long ago. Now I was on another, to be reunited with that same person, as Julie Wetherby.

And, as coincidence would have it, I found myself on a route I'd undertaken several times before, when I'd visited cousin Alice and her husband Mike. How strange that out of the whole country, they should live but a stone's throw away! And as the diesel trundled to a stop at the familiar rural railway halt, where they had in the past met me, I stared out into the car park. This time no-one waited there, and I wasn't getting off the train. My destination lay further down the track.

I felt mean and sad. But I couldn't face it; meeting these relatives, at a moment I could share with no other, wasn't an option. This was something I needed to do alone. And besides, there might even be a problem. Did Alice and brother Philip actually know I was adopted?

I'd always hoped they hadn't known and, until the last few years, truly believed that might be so. Although I didn't see them often, they were family to me, more so probably than I was to them, since they'd married and had children of their own. The fear that had stirred in me as a child was stronger now than ever. If they were to discover that I wasn't a blood relation – not 'one of them' – they might think I was a fake, hadn't told the truth. But what had my parents said to my aunt and uncle?

The more I thought about it, the more it seemed

probable that my mum and dad hadn't told them. Uncle Henry had been posted to Singapore not long before I came onto the scene, and Alice and Philip had spent much of their early years living abroad. It wasn't until the naval ball that I'd actually met them, and I had only seen them from time to time after that, during holidays from their respective boarding schools. Unlike Eva, on the other side of my family, with whom I had adoption in common, no-one on this side had ever mentioned the fact that I didn't share the same blood as theirs.

My concern over this question had begun to mount when, several years previously, I was helping Alice by wrapping a present for the wedding of Philip's younger daughter Kate, and making a pretty good job of it, so it appeared.

'You can see you're a Wetherby,' my cousin commented breezily.

I was flattered, since the tenacity and determination of our sibling parents was celebrated. The Wetherbys were good reliable stock. Got things done, faced adversity. Faced German bombs. But what did she mean? That as I'd grown up in the family environment I'd simply absorbed the characteristics? Or that she thought I really was a Wetherby? A real one. I said nothing, and a sense of unexplained business hovered over us.

* * *

My upbringing hadn't passed Alice and Philip unnoticed though. Several times Alice mentioned to me how, as a child, Mum had been overprotective of me. I knew it to be true of course; it had been a constant thorn in the side, the sort that led to the fear-driven invention of Mr. McDonald, and the sort that caused me to ask an indignant 'Who am I?' in the apple orchard all those years ago.

On one particular occasion we'd met up with Aunt Lorna, Uncle Henry and my cousins at the seaside. Judging from photographs, it was barely a year after the ball and Dad's time in hospital as the phoney Mr. McDonald. The menfolk had braved the grey-blue water first and dived into its foaming waves, swimming far out. Alice followed, picking her way over the sandy beach, which was peppered with small pebbles here and there. Then, waist deep, she took to the water like a mermaid, long blonde hair floating behind her.

Aunt Lorna remained behind, knitting contentedly, in the company of Brandy, the family's cocker spaniel, his lead tied to her deckchair. Meanwhile Mum busied herself with wrapping me in one of those homemade towelling garments with a hole in the top for the head, which pulled together over the shoulders by a drawstring. Bathing costumes on, hand in hand, the two of us made careful progress down the beach across the sand and pebbles.

I'd only recently learned to swim, a kind of dog paddle in the confines of the shallows, up and down, along by the seashore. But I loved it and wanted to remain in the water all afternoon, kicking and splashing. Mum stayed close, a little way out, sometimes floating on her back, sometimes breaking into a gentle breaststroke as she kept her eye on me.

'Time to get out!' she announced suddenly.

The others were still enjoying themselves in greater depths: Dad, Uncle Henry, Philip and Alice.

'It's not fair!' I shouted. 'I want to stay in!'

Mum was upon me, lifting me up by the straps of my costume. I struggled.

'Come out now Julie – you'll catch your death of cold.'

'Let me go!'

People were watching as I fought to free myself. Dad was watching now too, as well as Uncle Henry, Philip and Alice, treading water, and Aunt Lorna from her deckchair. Brandy barked, while Mum dragged me up the beach. I was crying.

And, as if to keep me company, the others had emerged from the sea, the fun spoiled, and were all drying themselves down with beach towels. No-one said anything, but I guessed what they were thinking: I was childish, and Mum was a fusspot. Only I was allowed to think that though, no-one else, and when Alice and Philip had both, on different occasions, recalled the incident which had clearly left its mark on the memory years later, I stood up for her. The woman who'd suffered two miscarriages, saved my life when I nearly died as a baby, and the woman who had witnessed the death of a golden-haired sister in the hospital bed beside her. She'd also felt an even greater responsibility towards me for yet another reason, about which I was yet to learn. The antithesis of abandonment was – after all – forgivable. Overprotectiveness.

After a handful of people alighted, the guard blew his whistle and the train edged away from the railway halt. How I wanted to pull the communication cord and request that the driver stop and let me off. It felt like an emergency. But as the platform narrowed towards a downward-sloping point merging with the side of the track, we gathered speed, and I knew I was committed. The next stop was the one at which I was due to get out, and as the train progressed through the familiar farmland scenery my heart beat faster and my stomach churned.

Was this how Joyce had felt over sixty years ago? The sense that there was no going back, that she had to go through with that to which she'd legally signed herself? There was no going back for me either, not after the part Angela and the adoption society had played in bringing this about.

Besides, I'd found a way to get round staying with Joyce and her partner – whose name, I'd discovered, was Arthur. Sarah, that old friend from teacher training college, had agreed to spend a few days away with me in a country house hotel, from where I'd been able to make this journey by train. We hadn't seen each other for ages; two of her children had fled the nest, and one was married. Husband Mark had given her his blessing to spend some time away and support me in my mission. I couldn't shrink from it now.

17

Reunion

Was it really happening? I asked myself, as I stared out of the train window. And why was I putting myself through all this? I imagined Sarah powering through several lengths of the heated indoor swimming pool back at the country club hotel, or perhaps undergoing an indulgent massage in the spa. I could have left this stuff all alone, simply carried on with my life as before, treated myself to some well deserved peace and quiet. It was too late, though, for such recriminations.

The countryside had begun to give way to the sporadic, picturesque, old red brick or timbered houses of passing villages, before the outskirts of a town came into view. It was a signal. One by one, my fellow passengers jumped up and reached overhead to remove luggage from racks. Then they made for the automatic doors which gave access to the narrow corridor that connected our carriage with the next. Reluctantly, I got up and followed them.

The train slowed as buildings grew taller: office blocks, high-rise apartments and a civic centre. Next, a railway platform. The driver braked until we came to a halt. I felt sick in the stomach. Doors whirred open, people alighted.

It was a short walk along the platform as I trailed behind the trickle of passengers towards steps which led to a footbridge. I'd rehearsed the scene so many times in my mind. Emerging from the station entrance by myself, I'd see a car with Arthur at the steering wheel and Joyce beside him in the front passenger seat, facing me. A cheery wave always followed, before Joyce got out and propelled herself towards me. We'd then throw ourselves into each other's arms in tight embrace.

And so my body went into action as if executing a military plan which had to be got through. I needed to make a good impression, be thought well of, show Joyce that I was worth it. I couldn't afford to get any of it wrong. My chest felt as if it was exploding as the other passengers climbed the steps and made their way across the overpass. An ordinary day for them most probably, routine.

The diesel pulled away from the platform, then rumbled forwards as I ascended the steps. The train passed beneath the concrete footbridge just as I turned onto it, distracting me. Why had I got off? Why hadn't I journeyed onwards to some semblance of safety after all? I stood there for a moment and watched as the back of the train's retreating rear carriage disappeared round a bend in the track.

I hadn't been prepared for her to be waiting there on

the bridge, alone. A tiny person, with the shadow of pale golden hair, dressed in a green quilted puffer jacket worn over a white, polo neck ribbed sweater and black trousers. The other passengers had walked on by, leaving just she and I standing there alone.

'Hello stranger,' she announced in an inappropriately semi-jocular tone of voice. Angela had warned me that Joyce could be gung-ho at times, a kind of act to cover up. I'd noticed it when talking to her on the phone: full of upbeat stories about how she'd braved this, overcome that, won an argument here, been congratulated there. Talk to impress. She had once shown the good grace to concede that what she'd done all those years ago was considered awful back then, but I wasn't sure whether it was a way to offer atonement or simply another feather in the cap, a kind of bravado – *'Just try and stop me!'* So, in a way, I was not entirely surprised by her greeting. But I was also disappointed. Deeply so.

Despite the warning sign, I flew into action without pause and threw my arms around her. Immediately I felt resistance, a tightening up of the body, arms barely making contact then falling loosely to the sides. My first mistake.

I followed Joyce across the bridge, a few steps behind. She wasn't quite as robust as I'd imagined, being more so in mind, perhaps, than in body. A kind of dogged determination.

She reached the top of the steps leading down to the

platform on the opposite side of the tracks from the one at which I'd got out. Placing one foot gingerly in front of the other she took the first step downwards, reaching out a hand to clutch the side rail to steady herself. Why had she bothered? Why hadn't she waited in the car with Arthur? It was what I'd expected her to do, and it occurred to me, even in that moment of utter bewilderment, that this was her way of making an effort. Something practical which displayed no emotion. Showing me the way.

'Can I help you?' I asked tentatively.

She shook her head firmly, mouth set in a hard line of concentration as she soldiered on down the steps. I was relieved; I didn't want to touch her again, feel her unyielding body shrink away from me.

Arthur was waiting in the car park. As we approached, he unwound himself from the driver's seat of a shiny, cream coloured Volvo estate, stepped out onto the tarmac and shook my hand. He wasn't at all like I'd expected. I'd imagined a hearty, stoutish man with iron grey hair and a rough dog-tooth patterned jacket. Instead he was tall and stooped with wisps of white hair brushed back off his forehead. He had a sensitive face with kind blue eyes behind rimless glasses, and lines carved deep into his pale skin. An open navy-blue sports jacket revealed a lemon cashmere sweater beneath. Instantly I liked him, just as I'd thought I might, even though he looked so different from the mental image I'd created. He signified a quiet stability.

'I'll sit in the back,' I said politely, and instantly admonished myself. Of course I was sitting in the back, there was no choice: Joyce had already opened the door giving access to the sumptuous cream leather upholstery of the rear seat. Obediently, I got inside, and sank down into its opulent folds, while Joyce took the seat immediately in front of me. Arthur got in beside her, banged shut the door and turned the key in the ignition. The luxurious vehicle purred into life.

I was nervous about being driven by a man in his late eighties, but Arthur seemed to know what he was doing. I was glad he and Joyce had both come to collect me; he provided a bolster between Joyce and myself, and an extra back-up to Sarah, who, in consultation with Angela, I'd planned would accompany me on a second visit the very next day. Eyes fixed upon the back of Joyce's pale gold head leaning against the headrest, I pinched myself. Was this really my birth mother, was this woman truly my own flesh and blood? There was nothing exciting at all about seeing someone to whom I was closely related, after all; she felt entirely alien to me.

As the journey progressed, the passing scenery helped to settle my still-churning stomach. Daffodils in gardens along the road raised their proud, golden-yellow trumpets towards the sun, tree branches were speckled with white and pale pink blossom, white clouds floated across a bright blue sky. Nature had choreographed it well, I thought, perhaps in anticipation of better things.

'Isn't this nice?' Joyce said, after a while.

'Yes, we're lucky with the weather,' Arthur replied.

She was reproachful. 'I meant – Arthur – isn't it nice having Julie with us!'

'Oh yes – I see, yes – yes – of course!'

Joyce was the mistress of understatement.

I enquired about the success of a recent minor operation she'd undergone. There was no reply.

'You'll have to speak louder – your mother's a bit deaf,' Arthur called over his shoulder.

Instantly a feeling of revulsion swept over me. Joyce had heard it too: Arthur's reference to our relationship. She turned her head to look at him sideways, as if deciding whether or not to say something.

I raised my voice, repeating my question.

'I've healed well, haven't I, Arthur?' she responded in an unnecessarily loud voice.

Arthur agreed that she had.

I was beginning to feel just a little sorry for him. This wasn't an easy situation to be dealing with, and I recalled how Arthur had apparently supported Joyce in her initial communications with me. He appeared to be a kind man, and for all the awkwardness and disappointingly anticlimactic reactions, I felt part of something I'd not experienced since a teenager. I was, all of a sudden, reminded of the times when Dad drove Mum and I to the beach at weekends. Days out, picnics, boat trips, strolls along the promenade, visits to the local seaside department store. Not that others hadn't included me in outings since, but now in the back of the Volvo, with the two of them sitting in the front, it almost seemed like old times. Even with the challenge of name labels and the stress of the occasion, I felt part of something, something that I belonged to. 'Life: Part Two' might actually be looking up.

My second mistake.

18

Fashioned in Images

Arthur and Joyce's residence was at the end of a cul-de-sac of modern, detached red brick houses, and commanded dramatic sea views, as Angela had relayed to me. But I was not entirely surprised, since I'd visited the place on Google Maps after Joyce's address had been revealed by Angela when, at last, my birth mother and I were writing to each other directly. It seemed surreal for the Volvo to be turning into the already familiar drive, up which I'd travelled several times, passing trim lawns, rockeries and double garages, while proceeding to the house at the very top.

Inside it, my bare feet sank into off-white wall to wall carpeting, which gave the already capacious dwelling an even greater sense of spaciousness. Nothing was spared in terms of quality. A lavish sunroom led off the dining room and afforded not only views of the English Channel, but also of a bank of peachy-pink and yellow roses, reminding me of the front lawn of Joyce's original home. There was much new teak furniture, like the modern oval table of the dining room, with its matching chairs. Above all, there was a preponderance of neutral shades, including the pale cream leather sofas of the sitting room, reminiscent of the

Volvo's interior, as though Arthur took an extension of his homestead with him wherever he went. It was like an upmarket show house, put together for the first time.

After a quick cup of coffee, Arthur took us out to lunch in an olde worlde pub. It was situated on the edge of a fishing village along the coast from where he and Joyce lived. Clearly the pair frequented it often and were well known amongst the staff. This meant we got good service.

Over the meal we chatted, and I found myself getting on well with Arthur. It appeared that he had one son called Jeremy, who was about ten years younger than me. Jeremy was married to Stella, an ex-beauty therapist. From what I could make out, Arthur and Joyce didn't greatly like her. The reason Stella had married Jeremy was for his money, they even claimed.

The pair had two children, a son and a daughter, on whom Arthur seemed to dote, even to the point of paying for them to go to boarding school. The money was wasted, Joyce pronounced several times; what was wrong with state education? I couldn't help but ponder why this information was being shared so openly with me at the meal table.

I offered to pay for our lunch, but Arthur wasn't having any of it. As we left the pub, and Joyce wandered on ahead of us to the car, I spontaneously patted him on the back and thanked him. I could tell he was pleased and understood that my gratitude was for far more than just lunch.

'What ship was your father on during the war?' Joyce asked, once we were settled in the big sitting room with its French windows, which like the sunroom, also afforded expansive views of the English Channel. A tanker drifted on the distant horizon. I was seated on the sofa, facing Joyce and Arthur who occupied the matching armchairs on either side of a fireplace filled with a dried hydrangea arrangement.

It was the aircraft carrier HMS *Illustrious*, I informed her. I explained how it had been involved in the famous Battle of Taranto off the tip of southern Italy. I also explained how it was badly damaged in the attack, before limping on its way from the Mediterranean out across the Atlantic to Norfolk, Virginia, for repairs. The information, supplied to me by Aunt May, soon after Dad's death, had been added to after I had researched the sea battle for myself in later years.

Joyce had shown an interest in him from the start – I knew that from Angela – because of the Portsmouth bombing raid. It had reminded her of another, without which the course of her life could well have been different. As mine could have been.

Arthur excused himself and said he was going to lie down, something he did every afternoon. It was usually while he was having his nap that Joyce now phoned me at weekends.

'I'll leave you to chat to your mother,' he announced, raising himself a trifle awkwardly out of his armchair.

I winced. Arthur had used that word again. 'Mother'.

Another silence ensued, during which Joyce reached out and touched his arm as he passed her by. Her lips were pursed. This was going to be a topic of conversation once I'd gone back to the county club, I could tell.

'He's done it several times,' she said, not looking me in the eye, as soon as Arthur disappeared. 'I hope you don't mind,' she added, sounding like the imperious headmistress at the end of the phone line the first time we'd spoken.

I did mind actually – I minded a lot. Although I was pleased that Arthur recognised the relationship as such, paradoxically I wished that he would not express it aloud. I was revulsed, just as I had been on the car journey from the station. It jarred with something deep down inside of me. And yet, I knew that it was Arthur's way of accepting me for who I truly was.

Suddenly I didn't know who I was at all.

'Just labels,' I murmured, trying not to look as though I was making a great deal of it, but at the same time avoiding Joyce's question. She looked relieved.

In front of me, on the glass top of a coffee table, lay several old photograph albums bound in scuffed leather.

'I put these out for you,' she said, lifting herself

slowly out of her armchair and moving over to sit beside me on the sofa.

I loved old photos, and realised it was Joyce's answer to the one I'd made for her, which sat beside them. A kind of retaliation, I couldn't help but wonder. '*That was your life – this was ours. This could have been yours.*'

There were pictures of my great grandparents, including the ones Maggie, the third cousin, had sent me. I hadn't let on about her, or the photographs. How could I explain that I'd found my third cousin on an ancestry notice board, that I'd had to tell her about my background?

There were others, of Joyce as a little girl. We did look a tiny bit alike, especially with our wavy hair, but we also looked quite different. Joyce's face was more determined, set in a firmer line, almost masculine. And there was the original Rose Keller, Joyce's mother. She was a handsome-looking woman and I remembered Angela's words. It was the only thing Joyce had been able to give me, her mother's name. I didn't resemble my namesake at all.

If only I could have seen photos of my birth father. But Desmond Gabbitas had made Joyce destroy them all, she'd told Angela, when I'd enquired earlier on. It was part of the marriage agreement.

'I went out with a boy for seven years,' Joyce began, as though picking up my thoughts, and repeated the information she had provided in her first letter to me. 'Charlie Dempsey.' So that's what she called him – Charlie. And she didn't refer to him as *'your father'*, as she'd done with my dad. Like in that first letter, she spoke from a distance, had removed herself from the direct connection I'd so hoped for.

'I nearly had an abortion.'

My heart stopped and my body turned stone cold like death itself. Joyce was talking about me as though I wasn't sitting there beside her. Did she have even the slightest inkling of what she was saying? What she was doing? – Perhaps I should be grateful that I'd been born at all, was still alive? – I sat in silence, unable to reply.

I returned to one of the heavy albums, still resting – uneasily – on my lap.

There were photos of people on my grandmother's side of the family: sisters, cousins, aunts. Again, I saw no likeness at all, and the more pages I turned and the more faces that stared back, the less I felt they had anything to do with me.

The other album contained photographs that were a little more up to date. There was a picture of Joyce and Desmond's wedding, and there were ones of Brenda. Her with Joyce. Her with Desmond and Joyce. By herself, growing up. Apart from colouring we didn't look much alike either. And her hair was dead straight. I particularly hated the photo of her with Joyce. A little girl, about two I reckoned, the same age as me in the portrait. A copy, framed, was displayed on a shelf, just out of reach, both mother and child smiling at the camera. The whole thing was mightily unfair.

There were other photos too. Of a man and woman who appeared in a number of them, along with a young boy. They also appeared in group photos with Desmond, Joyce and Brenda. I took a closer look. The man was tall, fair haired, and slightly stooped.

'That looks like Arthur,' I said, pointing to one particular shot.

'It *is* Arthur,' Joyce replied. 'And that's his wife, Polly,' she added, indicating a tiny woman beside him, with dark brown permed hair. 'She and I were friends before she married Arthur. She died twelve years ago.'

So Arthur and Joyce had known each other for a long time and, both widowed, had thrown in their lot together.

'And that's Jeremy.' Joyce stabbed her finger onto the picture of the boy, dark-haired like Polly.

My eyes strayed to a card on the mantelpiece. '*Happy Mother's Day*', the words read, above a picture of a teddy bear with its arm around another. Was this some kind of crass joke? Or had Joyce simply not thought – again; been unable to place herself in my shoes? Perhaps this was what I deserved, a payback for meddling with things from the past that were better left alone.

'Did you like the portrait?' I now dared to enquire.

Joyce hadn't mentioned it at all, and there was no sign of it anywhere.

She sighed, placed her head on one side and gave me a pitying smile.

'Not very much,' she said.

My heart exploded, tears stung the corners my eyes. How could she? The picture my parents had painted of me!

I took a deep breath.

'Would you prefer I took it away, then?'

At this, Joyce seemed abashed.

'Could I think about it?' she asked.

But I'd already made up my mind.

'Of course,' I lied.

'There's something I need to explain,' she began, then stopped. Arthur had returned from his rest.

'That must have taken a good deal of time and thought,' he said, nodding towards the album I'd made for Joyce.

19

Trashed

I sat in the back seat of Arthur's Volvo, among the folds of soft cream leather, my sorrow so great I thought I would burst. On the surface, the visit had been a success but, underneath, it was a raging failure. I longed to get to the railway station, say my temporary farewells and disappear.

After what seemed like an age, and a great deal of silence as the country route we'd travelled that morning reversed itself, Arthur turned into the station forecourt and brought the car to a halt. He got out and opened the back door for me. We kissed on the cheek and he took my hand.

'You can come and stay whenever you like,' he said, glassy-eyed. 'You don't have to go to a hotel in the future, you know. And you can have any room in my house you want.'

The house – yes – it belonged to him. After returning from his afternoon nap, he'd prepared tea for the three of us. It comprised a tray bearing three china cups on saucers, a matching teapot and a plate bearing neatly cut slices of fruitcake, which he'd placed down on the coffee table. This was his house, and he was master of it. Joyce had sat in the armchair she'd seemingly appropriated for herself, like a presiding queen bee, waited on hand and foot.

'I'm a kept woman,' she'd joked.

Standing beside the Volvo, I thanked him. Arthur was kind, like a new father figure. But I didn't want to dwell on that. It was too painful, and it wouldn't have taken much to reduce me to tears. He helped Joyce out of the front passenger seat, then quietly left us to it and got back inside the car.

'Thank you for coming,' she said, standing before me, head on one side once more. 'See you tomorrow.'

'Goodbye,' I muttered, trying to hide the quiver in my voice.

I pecked her on the cheek and without looking back marched into the railway station, then waited alone on the platform for the train to arrive and convey me to freedom. It was on time, and after boarding, I entered an almost empty railway carriage, relieved that I could shed any tears in private.

I'd spent quite a while deliberating on which way round to organise my two visits to Joyce. Since I'd gone to all the trouble of fixing up the holiday with Sarah, I'd wanted to make the most of it. And to introduce an old friend to my birth mother seemed appropriate in the circumstances. Sarah was, indeed, my backup. Besides, I wanted her to meet Joyce, get her opinion. She'd known my mum, after all. And she'd known about my background ever since college days.

I'd wondered if I should take her with me for the first meeting, then cast off the inflatable arm bands and go alone the second time. The more I'd thought about it, the more I was reminded of that very first railway journey when Joyce had conveyed me to London. Somehow it had seemed fitting to be reunited with her alone. To have someone else there at the start hadn't felt right at all.

But to know that Sarah was waiting for me back at the hotel was reassuring. Disconsolately I stared out of the carriage window at the passing farmland, while hot tears trickled from the corners of my eyes. Once more the train stopped at the familiar backwater halt, once more the car park was empty.

I had, to some extent, been prepared for Joyce and the way she was. It didn't make it any better, though. I was a child, craving love and affection. That's what it's like for adoptees – cut off from their biological mother soon after birth – no matter what the circumstances. A trauma so great, ingrained deep within, brought to light by psychological study. I know it to be so. Age is irrelevant.

No-one alighted, no-one got on. And as the train pulled away from the halt, I thought of Alice and wondered what she'd make of me passing that way on my secret mission, without even telling her. Although the subject of adoption hadn't ever been raised between us, there were certain things we *had* discussed about the past. The Portsmouth bombing raid for one, and Aunt May's shocking disclosure. Alice had raised her eyebrows in that arched, questioning manner she was so good at, developed in childhood, wondering why my mum hadn't mentioned my dad's first wife at all. She perhaps concluded, as I had done, that I was being sheltered from events that were better not known about.

Yes – Dad's first wife Rachel had died in a cupboard under the stairs, she confirmed. Yes – she knew that her father, my Uncle Henry, had sent a wartime telegram and that my dad had never received it. There were others things she knew as well, she said. I didn't dare ask about these, and she didn't expound further.

'How was it?' Sarah asked cautiously, as I entered her hotel bedroom.

I closed the door behind me, dropped my shoulder bag down onto the floor, and burst into tears.

'I don't like her.'

We hugged each other tight.

'I was afraid it might be like this,' she said. 'All this mush on TV about happy family reunions, it gives such a distorted view of the thing. Sugary sweet – everything lovely in the garden.'

'I suppose sometimes it is,' I replied forlornly, sitting on the edge of her bed.

'Do you still want to go back?' she asked.

I explained about Arthur, how he'd been so kind to me. And about the portrait.

'Maybe Joyce will change her mind,' Sarah suggested.

But I wasn't going to give Joyce the chance. Something told me I needed to get the portrait out of her house.

Next morning we went to the supermarket, where I purchased a roll of black plastic sacks. And although it took longer because of traffic congestion, Sarah drove us to Arthur and Joyce's this time. Again, Arthur took us out to lunch at their usual local, and things seemed more relaxed as a foursome. It was only when Arthur referred to Joyce as my mother once more, that the atmosphere changed while she bristled in momentary silence.

Before our arrival, she'd phoned Angela, so she said, told her how well things had gone after our first meeting. Did Joyce really think that, or was she just trying to construct something convenient to believe? Maybe that's how she'd lived her life, ever since Charlie Dempsey. Constructing her own version of events.

Both Joyce and Arthur made Sarah welcome. They seemed used to socialising and slipped easily into a role that perhaps reflected, to some extent at least, the novelty of their comparatively recent and apparently successful partnership. It was as if the pair of them were playing newly-marrieds, even though they hadn't tied the knot.

It was a home in which Joyce played the part of lady of the manor with great aplomb. She gardened, and cooked home-grown fruit and vegetables – the latter tended by Arthur, as he reminded her. They shopped and entertained together. It was also a home in which Joyce put on buffet lunches as fundraising events for the local branch of the Conservatives, as she trumpeted. And one in which she presided at, and catered for, the tri-annual family luncheon parties, about which I was to hear a lot.

Joyce showed Sarah round the four upstairs bedrooms. Downstairs, Arthur spoke of the off-white, deep pile carpets which the pair of them had chosen to create a sense of flowing unity, and how they'd also chosen the oval teak table with care. He went on to explain that he'd sold the antique furniture which had filled his old farmhouse. This was clearly the home he'd shared with Polly, although he didn't say so.

'We only eat here on special occasions,' he announced to Sarah, sweeping a forearm in the air over the table's well-polished surface. 'It's where our two families sit when they come together,' he added.

The corners of my eyes smarted, a knot formed in my stomach. In that moment I might as well have not been there, might as well have not existed. Sarah nodded politely.

* * *

Arthur took Sarah off to show her the garden, while Joyce resumed the same place beside me on the sofa as the previous day. Snatching some private time with me, she spoke of Charlie's mother, Ellen Dempsey. How she'd hated her, and how the feeling had been mutual. I wasn't entirely surprised.

When Arthur returned from the garden with Sarah, he went upstairs to rest. After seeking permission, I showed my friend the album I'd made for Joyce. And I showed her the photographs of Brenda, when Joyce was temporarily out of the room. Sarah lay an understanding arm on my shoulder.

'Do you like that picture?' Joyce asked Sarah, once she'd returned, pointing to a reproduction print of a Lowry painting mounted on the sitting room wall. 'Brenda bought it for me.'

Sarah said she did. It was my cue, my body already on fire.

'Talking of pictures – would you like to give me the portrait?' I asked, leaping to my feet. I'd fixed a nasty smirk on my face. Reaching into my shoulder bag, I brought out a single, folded, black plastic sack. 'I can remove it now,' I stated, although this was intended more in the nature of an offer.

Joyce was taken aback, I could tell. I was pleased.

'I don't know,' she said. 'I'll go and get it. Ask your friend what she thinks.'

Joyce disappeared, while Sarah and I exchanged dubious glances. A moment later she reappeared with the picture, the subject's face forward, enfolded by an arm. Her golden-haired child, held in an uncaring embrace.

My pulse raced, my face grew hot.

'It's sweet,' Sarah said. She'd never before seen the pensive little girl with the pale gold locks in the emerald green dress.

'Do you really think so?' Joyce asked, placing it down on the sofa, then stepping back to regard it once more. 'Personally, I think it looks like a doll.' She pronounced this statement with a certain disdain.

'Then you won't have to look at it anymore,' I retaliated crisply, opening up the plastic sack. Sarah took it and held it open, while swiftly I placed the portrait inside. A sense of sad relief washed over me. I hadn't really wanted to part with it at all.

20

The Aftermath

I dragged my suitcase into the hallway of my apartment and closed the door behind me. Tired after my journey and deflated from my time away, all I wanted to do was boil the kettle and make myself a cup of tea. The phone rang. I was tempted not to answer, but found myself lifting the receiver to my ear.

'You're home,' she said.

'I've just walked in through the door,' I replied.

'Thank you for coming.'

Joyce was clinging on for dear life, I could tell. She'd already tried her best to ground me before I'd left the hotel and bade my farewells to Sarah.

'A volcano has erupted in Iceland,' she'd announced when she'd called my mobile. 'You should come and stay here; the flights will probably be cancelled.'

My flight had certainly been cancelled, and I'd taken the coach home instead. Now I thanked Joyce for having me, and felt like a fraud. I knew what I'd really like to say, but held it back; I couldn't get Arthur's kindness out of my mind. But inside my suitcase, protected by bubble wrap, was the rejected portrait of that little girl.

'Jeremy phoned,' she said. 'He'd tried Arthur several

times when we were out to lunch the day your friend was here. He wanted to know where Arthur and I were.'

I couldn't for the life of me see where all this was leading to, and let her carry on.

'Arthur explained we were at the restaurant with friends. Jeremy kept on at him, asking who we were with.'

A cold hand tightened itself around my solar plexus. Reality was dawning. Not only the aftermath of an anticlimactic meeting with my birth mother and all the baggage that came with that, but another matter, which, just then, I sensed was going to be much, much worse.

'Did Arthur tell him?' I ventured.

'No – he couldn't do that. You see, it's complicated.'

Why did it have to be complicated? Nothing had been mentioned to Angela about problems with the birth family, or associated members of it. We'd been given to understand that Joyce's metaphorical house was in order, before going ahead with the reunion. Granted, Brenda hadn't yet surfaced, and I was unsure of things where she was concerned, yet I'd also felt relieved. Dealing with a younger sister that Joyce had kept when I'd been relinquished would have been too much to bear, just then. Seeing photographs of her was enough.

'I don't understand,' I said.

'There was something I was going to tell you, the day you came alone,' Joyce continued. 'But Arthur returned from his rest.'

I remembered now.

'I did, however, tell you that Polly and I were friends from long ago.'

I also remembered that, yes, recalled the short, dark-haired lady behind a much younger Arthur, and the little boy, so like her, by her side.

'Polly had a baby girl back in the early fifties when she was still single, and I was her midwife. She had to have the child adopted.' Joyce paused. 'We became friends, and I told her about my own experience. Before she married Arthur, I said she must tell him the truth. Just as I told Desmond the truth.'

This was news.

'And?'

'It was as well. Polly's brother Ralph knew about the baby. He was a nasty piece of goods. One day, after Jeremy was born, he phoned Polly and asked her to lend him some money. He threatened to let on to Arthur about Polly's past if she didn't pay up. Instead she got Arthur to call him back and he told him where to get off!'

Joyce paused again, before continuing.

'Having a backup plan is essential in such circumstances. One never knows, once the truth is out, what people are inclined to go and do! The matron at the nursing home I was working at threatened to have me struck off the nursing register, once.'

I assumed this was when Joyce was expecting Brenda. I'd noticed on the copy of her birth certificate that she was born at the same nursing home address as the one Joyce had provided the authorities, revealed in some correspondence in my file. Doubtless she had used Desmond as a bargaining point, a GP whom, come hell or high water, she eventually intended to marry.

'I presume Jeremy doesn't know about the past,' I said, my tone matter-of-fact.

'Absolutely not! Arthur didn't want to expose Polly's shame when she was alive, let Jeremy know he has a half sister. And since Polly's death he's wanted to be loyal to her memory.'

I didn't know what to say, since I needed to mask something I might later regret. Anger bubbled inside. All I knew was that I was shrouded in the same shame as Polly's illegitimate baby and it hurt like hell.

Joyce went on.

'So – you see – Arthur doesn't want Jeremy to know about you.'

I began to sense where this might be going.

'After Polly's death, Arthur and I started to visit each other. Of course, ever since Polly married him, we were friends. Eventually, we both agreed that living alone was a pain as you get older, so we threw in our lot together. I helped Arthur clear out the old farmhouse where he and Polly had lived most of their married life. What a mess it was in! Arthur bought this place where we are now, because it's easy to get down here from London for both Jeremy and Brenda.'

It explained even more the newness of the house, with its expensive contents straight from the retailer. A fresh start where the shadows of the past could be kept at bay. The only hint given of it lay in the contents of albums and the framed photographs of people whose eyes stared into an unspecified distance, seemingly avoiding me. Brenda with Joyce, and Brenda's son – Daniel he was called – kitted out in graduation robes, scrolled certificate clutched proudly in hand. Dark, Spanish-looking. There were pictures of dogs that Joyce and Arthur had independently owned in the past: boxers, Labradors, a German shepherd with a dark coat that had reminded me of Titus. And there were the two much-adored grandchildren on Arthur's side, a girl and a boy pictured together at the seaside, just as I'd been pictured with Alice and Philip on the sandy beaches of our youth, with Brandy the cocker spaniel. Humans and their animals doing the most ordinary of things in the most extraordinary of circumstances.

'Jeremy was up in arms when he thought that Arthur intended to remarry. Stella was yapping at his heels over money, their inheritance, and was begging him to ask Arthur not to forget the children. As if he would!'

They'd already bled him dry by the sound of it, what with school fees, I thought. But Arthur did not appear to be short of money. Surely there was plenty to go round for everyone.

'He got us all together, Jeremy did. A meeting with Brenda and I. Arthur caved in, he adores his son. He was a late, long-awaited child. And much adored. Jeremy made himself clear; Arthur is putty in his hands you see. So it was agreed that Arthur and I would simply live together, and that I could stay on in the house if he goes first.'

In the saga's momentary gap, I remained silent.

'Then, after I die, the property gets left to Jeremy. But if Jeremy gets to hear about you – about my past – he might well make things difficult. He might even point the finger; at the best, make jokes. He could even turf me out, say that I was an unfit person to live on in his father's house.'

'I see,' I replied sourly.

And in a way, I did see. I saw that Joyce was intent on preserving the reputation she'd created for herself, and I guessed that my existence tarnished it, rocked the boat. I didn't like the sound of this Jeremy. How could I ever accept Arthur's kind invitation to stay under his roof in any bedroom I liked? It was a ridiculous fantasy.

'And he doesn't know about Brenda – that Desmond wasn't her father. We never talked about it when they were young, and we aren't going to start talking about it now.'

We'd never talked about it either, Joyce and I. Like so many things, this detail had been skimmed over, implicit in non-annunciation. It had been reliant on

Angela, my file, and the internet. The way things had always been, out of habit: unmentioned, unexplained.

Excusing myself, I said goodbye, and replaced the receiver. I didn't even bother to fill the kettle, but reached for a bottle of sherry instead.

I poured some into a glass, swigged it down, unlocked the suitcase and removed the portrait layered in bubble wrap. Ripping off the cover, I revealed the vulnerable subject beneath. The child with the golden curls and the pensive look. She stared away off centre as though she saw something no-one else could see, could sense something no-one else understood. And now I understood both her – Rose Keller made Julie Wetherby – and her sorrow.

Just then, the polite, protective cloak surrounding me was ripped apart. Why had I landed myself in this present-day melee of intrigue, dishonesty and pain?

There was only one thing for it.

21

Someone Else's Child

'I'm throwing in the sponge!' I announced, when I phoned Sarah after she got home. Breathlessly, with hurried words punctuated by bouts of sobbing, I retold Joyce's story to her. My anger, my frustration, my tears.

'That's terrible,' Sarah said after I'd finished and she'd had time to digest the contents of the tale. In the background I could hear Mark clattering pots and pans. He was now the cook of the household, and for a moment I felt that I was pouring my troubles onto a quiet haven of marriage in retirement: the path of least resistance, when each partner does their own thing without the diversion of work or children.

I forged on.

"I've done what I set out to do – met Joyce, said 'hello' – it's all I asked for. She – they – should have accepted it at that."

'It *was* all you asked for,' Sarah agreed. 'And I appreciate how you feel, Julie, it's a real let-down. But maybe you just need to see past Joyce's defensiveness – underneath, there's a woman hurting so much.'

I wasn't having any of it.

'*She* may be hurting – but what about me? How does she think I must feel?' I demanded angrily, aware that Sarah didn't deserve my wrath, especially after being such a loyal friend.

'Joyce is probably feeling guilty too,' Sarah replied quietly.

'All they need to do is tell the truth, for God's sake!' I roared through bitter tears. 'They're just perpetuating the past with all the lies and secrets. It sounds like a rerun of my adoption file. Hush-hush, hidden away, dirty.'

A pan crashed to the kitchen floor. Sarah made an aside to Mark; he laughed it off.

'Perhaps you should phone your counsellor,' she suggested.

Sarah was right, I knew I should – it was no good piling my troubles onto others, they had their own lives to lead. How could they be expected to fully understand, in any case?

My reunion with Joyce had indeed been so much more than a mere 'hello,' about which, I now recalled, I'd assured her no-one else need know. How I rued those words!

Yet Joyce hadn't played fair. On the one hand she'd agreed to meet me, but both she and Arthur had also made inclusive noises. The attempt to ground me after the Icelandic volcano had erupted, the repeated invitation to stay. Those hadn't been the terms I'd offered, but if it was what they insisted on, then I wasn't prepared to be kept under wraps, slinking around beneath the radar.

And she hadn't come clean and told Angela about the family complications; instead she'd allowed me to be exposed to it unprepared. As if I'd feel okay with all the photographs, the Mother's Day card still on display, and the portrait rebuff! Feel okay with being told that I still had to be a secret! Why couldn't they all grow up, tell the truth? But they were from another generation, I reminded myself, old enough to have cover-ups carved deeply into their being. Old enough to have lived years of things being locked away, pretending that none of it had happened.

'It was a disaster!' I wailed to Angela down the phone.

'I expect Joyce didn't tell us about the problems because she suspected that you might never have gone to meet her.'

'And Arthur was so kind, and yet all this is to do with him!' I responded.

Gone were my hopes of family integration, being accepted into a unit. I had no real immediate family since my parents' respective deaths, no husband and no children, put off by what I'd grown up to believe. And now that distant spark of hope had dwindled to almost nothing.

Angela's voice was gentle but firm.

"It's up to you, Julie. You can decide to continue your interactions with Joyce, or you can just walk away, mission accomplished."

Put like that, my choice was a stark one. But Angela was right. Only I could make that decision. Gone was the initial hand-holding offered me by the adoption society. They were there for life, my counsellor had once said, as a support. But after the intermediary stages they were really there as a sounding board, and they couldn't tell me what to do – I realised that. Yet we were still bobbing up and down in the wake of the turbulence.

'I can phone Joyce,' Angela suggested. 'See what she has to say. It's normal to have a follow-up call after a first meeting.'

Maybe the last, I thought to myself.

'Don't forget Julie – adoptees feel a deep sense of rejection. This will have made things feel so much worse for you.'

Didn't I know that? But I needed reminding. I shouldn't beat myself up for losing it. And I'd kept things together pretty well when visiting Joyce and Arthur, outwardly. I was bound to feel like this, I told myself, even without the problems of Arthur's family.

The phone rang again next day. Angela.

'I've spoken to Joyce,' she said.

'What did she have to say?'

'There seem to be a number of complications. Principally money.'

My stomach felt like lead. I'd made it clear from the start that this wasn't about gold digging. The social workers in Diane's department had indeed questioned my sudden desire to search, which, they were assured, was not associated with that root of all evil.

'Why now?' they'd demanded.

How could I have explained the revelation that had struck me on waking that January morning? The voice in my head commanding me to search, telling me to find my roots before it was too late. Now I wished I hadn't heard it at all.

'Joyce and Arthur are both very taken with you,' Angela continued. 'And Arthur wants to leave you something.'

My gut twisted. I didn't want money from Arthur, especially in the circumstances. But I did need love – from both of them – but not at the price of lies.

I uttered a grunt of disgust.

Angela went on.

'That's why he doesn't want Jeremy to know about you. In case he contests the will.'

I needed to walk away fast from them all. I hadn't wanted any of this, the immense pain, the injustice of being kept a secret. Most of all I didn't want to be involved in money struggles. By implication Arthur's son and his greedy wife Stella would see me as an interloper, someone with unscrupulous motives.

'I don't think I can accept,' I said. 'This wasn't what I'd wanted, a possible fracas over a will.'

'But if that's what Arthur wishes, Julie, perhaps you should. He's perfectly entitled to do whatever he wants with his money, it shouldn't be up to Jeremy.'

I supposed Angela was right. But at the same time I was angry, because I'd entered into something nasty. I might even have to take precautionary measures when the time came. Yet maybe not, perhaps the topic of Arthur's will was simply a red herring, a distraction from other issues? It might even be designed as a way to bait me in a desperate attempt to keep me in touch with them both, when in fact Arthur felt unable to leave me anything at all. Whatever was going on, I so wished that I'd ignored that summoning voice in my head.

I also wanted to know what Joyce had to say about the portrait, but I guessed the reason, which Angela confirmed. She couldn't hang it on the walls, questions would be asked, people would want to know the identity of the person in it.

Why not tell them! Why not be proud in public? Of me, who I was, Joyce's elder daughter. This was getting nearer the truth, I was sure of it. I recalled how she hadn't liked the portrait, how that had hurt the most. I voiced my feelings; Angela sympathised.

I thought of the dog-eared, faded colour photograph of me in the sunbonnet, kneeling in the water's shallows as a toddler. How Joyce had shed tears when she'd looked at it, imagining herself holding the beach towel. It was what had started it all off.

'How could anyone dislike a portrait of a little girl at the seaside?' I then asked.

'Because you were someone else's child – not hers – that's why,' Angela said. 'The portrait was of your parents' child, commissioned by them. It was too painful.'

I saw it clearly. Rose Keller made manifest in Julie Wetherby. The child as my mum and dad had wanted me to be. Suddenly, I was glad that it was too painful for Joyce. It was what she deserved. Now I was resolved to take the next step.

'Think very carefully, Julie,' Angela warned when I told her, 'don't do anything you might later regret.'

22

Another Landmark Birthday

Had not my sixty-first birthday been just around the corner, I might have finished with Joyce right then. Having a birthday which I could share with her held significance though; it was the first since I was born. And it was sixteen years since I'd received a card, on the last birthday I'd spent with Mum.

Accepted, most people can only share a birthday with one mother, and after that person has passed away, only memories remain. But when you have two mothers you have to go through the pain of maternal death twice, whatever the circumstances. This could be the last chance to share that special day with the person who had brought me into the world, the person from whom I'd been wrenched away at two weeks old, only to be reunited just briefly on a train journey to London three weeks later. The person who, beneath the layers of cruel defence, by her own admission, had once emitted faint glimmers of something better.

The reason for my feelings, I'd already begun to suspect, was the recognised trauma of separation from an infant's biological mother. It is indeed huge, the wound inflicted so deep it can never truly be healed. The consequences can be recognised, addressed, but not stamped out. I knew it back then, even before I was to research these matters in earnest. I'd felt it in my very being, when that dark, dark place was first exposed. Then again, upon the reading of my adoption file, and still further when I looked at Joyce's sparkling womanly young face in the black and white photograph. A familiarity absorbed, unconsciously present all my life. Such things can be read about yet not known. I'd known it before I read of it. And I know it still now.

Ever present is the belief that once an adopted child goes to a good home, all the wrongs are cancelled out. My friends believed it, especially Sarah. She'd known my mum, had known that I was adopted, attempted to console me in my distress after the meeting with Joyce and Arthur. Well meant, it was as if she was trying to wipe away both my tears and what had happened during my recent visit, in order to make things better. I knew it wasn't so, and realised that I was in danger of exploding at anyone who might think otherwise.

It isn't so – just isn't! The rows, distress and shame absorbed into the cells of the growing fœtus cannot make it right. Neither can the heartbreak of lying in a wicker basket placed on the floor of a private room in a nursing home. Nor the osmosis from mother to child of plans made for relinquishment, the reasons she – that child – cannot be kept. Next, sensing the uncertainties of foster parents with whom she is lodged and with whom a bond is forming. Will they get to keep her, and, if not, what will become of her?

It is remembered, in the body, it remains there forever. It explains why the Julie Wetherbys of this world throw their metaphoric toys out of the pram, residues of real ones, like the china doll presented by an aunt who plays the role of wicked fairy godmother. I know, because it happened. I threw the doll Aunt Astrid had given me onto the floor. The doll survived, chipped and scarred, just as the child did, and when, in later years the latter asked why the former had a broken arm, she was told of the incident by her mum.

It also explains the childhood temper tantrums, when things didn't appear to go Julie Wetherby's way. When grown-ups thought it was better that she should be locked in her bedroom at night with a chamber pot, in case she tried to run away again: overprotected. When grown-ups pretended, for whatever good reason, that the child's 'real' mother had died. Why, when she asked who she really was – and no satisfactory answer could be given – she suffered torment.

I just couldn't do it, break with Joyce, even though it might have been deserved. Already I knew of sadness and regret. And guilt. Angela's words of warning rang in my ears.

The memories still haunt me. That day, a week

before my eighteenth birthday. A grumpy teenager studying for 'A' levels, the exams coming up in a matter of weeks. And to complicate matters I'd been sent home from school with the worst head cold ever. I was confined to my room, told to stay there since it was imperative my germs didn't spread to Dad. He was in the dining room, lying on a makeshift bed, set up there as he couldn't climb the stairs.

He mightn't have even survived until then if the element in the kettle hadn't failed one morning. While waiting for the water to heat in a saucepan the pain from a coronary thrombosis spread fast and furious across his chest when normally he would have been driving to work. And now, just as a slow recovery appeared to be taking place, I was isolated, separated from him.

My meals were served to me on a tray by Mum, her nose and mouth covered in a white handkerchief folded in a triangle and tied in a knot at the back of her head. She hadn't been at all happy when Dad was discharged from St. Jude's on Dindevan, the anticoagulant drug capable of causing hemorrhagic stroke if not correctly controlled. Could the GP come daily to check on him? she'd wanted to know. It wasn't possible, the doctor said, Dad would have to take the drug as prescribed without such regular medical check ups.

I'd been in my bedroom for a whole day when I heard comings and goings downstairs. The front door opening, Mum's urgent voice. I ran to the window and saw our GP rushing up the drive armed with some sinister-looking, box-shaped medical equipment. I knew it was serious.

I stayed in my room; no-one came near. Eventually, Mum climbed the stairs to break the news. A terrible headache had led on to Dad finally losing consciousness. A friend of Mum's from church was coming to stay the night with me while she went to the hospital with him.

Light was fading fast. Just before nightfall I heard the doctor rush out of the house. I watched from my bedroom window as he ran down the drive to stand in the road waving a torch at the approaching ambulance. It drew up outside our house, the driver stopping to reverse the vehicle up the drive, which was on a slope. The rear doors opened and I withdrew from the window.

Next there was the thunder of the ambulance crew's feet stomping through the hallway into the dining room. Moments later, against the friend's advice, I crept to the top of the stairs, a silent, unseen observer. Below me one of the ambulance crew appeared from the dining room, pulling a collapsible canvas stretcher chair into the narrow hallway, towards the porch. Slumped in it, chin on chest, was Dad, his skin the colour of grey ash. His eyes were closed. The kind, gentle face that, despite the often jocular exterior, had always borne the scars of matters deep and unexplained, now lolled to one side onto his chest in doomed unconsciousness. Behind him, another member of the crew emerged, holding the handles of the chair, as slowly the dismal entourage disappeared through the front door.

Later that same night came the phone call I hadn't wanted to hear.

As I returned once more to the photograph album of my youth, I felt guilt at being the horrible, rebellious adolescent, ungrateful at times, wrought in the fires of adoption. If only I could have that time again, put things right with Dad, tell him how much I loved him, how truly grateful I was for his desire to adopt me.

If only I could have that time again with Mum. I recalled the last birthday spent together, when she'd paced around the care home, anxious, yet sufficiently compos mentis to know the date, clutching my birthday card until I'd arrived. It was signed, as always, *'Your ever loving parent.'* How she must have pondered on my birth every year the day came round again, just as I had always done when I read her words.

I couldn't risk feeling bad again, over Joyce. And when I explained it to Angela, she told me how Joyce had phoned her, thinking I might not want the present she had planned for me. It arrived, the silver necklace, on my sixty-first birthday, accompanied by a card with a picture of a Siamese kitten. With it came her phone call, wishing me a happy birthday for the first time ever.

23

Private Property

Good relations politely restored, Joyce and I kept in touch by phone that summer. I began to look forward to her calls, which came mainly at weekends, and the invitation to stay arose again. Still I couldn't get Arthur's kindness out of my mind and heart, and wished, so fervently, that the situation with Jeremy didn't exist. Despite this, I finally accepted the original invitation to stay, and arranged a three night visit in August.

But there were other things that spurred me on as well, not least Joyce's own birthday in June. It was the first time I was able to wish her many happy returns. Card and gift despatched, I received a call from her.

'A year ago my birthday horoscope confirmed matters,' she said, out of the blue.

'In what way?' I asked, riveted.

'It said that someone from the past would come into my life in six months.'

My spine tingled. Six months on from June was December, the month when the social workers found Joyce, and Diane first made contact with her.

'I know what that is, I thought to myself!' Joyce added.

It explained her remark to Diane, reported back to me via Angela, and a similar comment she'd made to my counsellor, when Joyce had first phoned her in January. I didn't quite know what to say, and let her continue.

'I had a near-death experience after I fell on the ice at the start of last year and was rushed to hospital. It seemed like a dream – being in a dark tunnel – light was shining at the far end.'

I could hardly believe what I was hearing.

'In January?'

'Yes, January. A figure was standing there, silhouetted against the light. And I heard a voice. Whoever it was told me to go back, said that someone was looking for me. I began to get better after that.'

I believed in such things, had experienced them myself. Strange dreams about people only to discover they'd just passed on, voices communicating with me, like Mum's, on the day she died. And my Dad's, in a maths exam, weeks after the fateful day in April, willing me on, telling me I could do it. The voice commanding me to search that January morning was, without doubt, the same one she'd heard. We were destined to come together like this, and underneath the crusty layers that hid Joyce's heart from the world, I sensed a kind woman who loved me. Someone who was deeply spiritual, in her own way. I had to hang on in there, make this work somehow, however difficult it might prove to be.

* * *

Flights and train tickets booked, the time to visit Joyce and Arthur grew closer. Angela was delighted that things were looking up for us, the only cloud on the horizon being Jeremy. I so hoped he wouldn't turn up while I was staying. One day a letter arrived from Joyce, bearing a south-west London postmark. It was where he lived. When I asked Joyce if she'd been there, my worst suspicions were confirmed. Jeremy had visited, seen some mail on the hall table and said he'd post it. Supposing he'd seen my name and address, wondered who I was? These days it was all too easy to google someone, get an insight into them. And why hadn't Joyce been more careful?

Soon I found the answer.

'If you meet any of my golfing friends, I'll introduce you as a Merriman cousin,' she announced, sounding pleased at her bright idea. The Merrimans were a branch of the family on her mother's – Rose Keller senior's – side. I'd discovered them during the ancestry search, had been confronted by them in the dull black and white photos of Joyce's album.

I didn't like this at all. Lying was something I wasn't prepared to be party to. But it was more than that. The idea clashed violently with that part of the younger me inside that still existed. The abandoned child, acting up.

'Baby Rage' – I'd heard it referred to in my read-

ings about adoption. It appeared that I was not alone in experiencing these feelings; it was a symptom that affects adult adoptees, no matter what age they are. The remnants of childhood. A china doll once more thrown from the pram.

Yes, I was angry at Joyce although I didn't say so to her face. I was shocked at what she'd suggested and the fact that she thought I'd be okay with it. And I was angry at myself because in that moment of shock I'd found myself agreeing, all because I still so desired to be part of her life – to be accepted.

Angela, as usual, took the flack. She did her best to convey to Joyce how I felt. But there was no way of telling that Joyce understood, could see things from my perspective. And yet, a still, small voice told me that deep down she did. After my visit that April, she'd admitted to Angela that she had forgotten to hide the framed photographs. And as for the albums – there were pictures of Brenda everywhere! How awful that must have made me feel! she'd exclaimed. If only she'd been able to communicate those things directly to me, had been able to address them in some way.

Clearly Joyce was someone who said things, opened her big mouth at the most inappropriate of times, then thought about it afterwards. How many people had she alienated in her life? I wondered. Ellen Dempsey, most certainly. Even her father – my grandfather – Robert Keller, had told her that her thoughtlessness would one day get her into a whole lot of trouble, a fact that she did once manage to admit to me on the phone.

I so hoped we wouldn't meet any of her friends, or Jeremy. Yet in a way, I realised, I didn't really want them to know who I was either. It was actually none of their business. I could do without the explanations, the whisperings behind our backs, the private past trampled over – dissected. It was my property alone. But I didn't want to lie, there'd been too many untruths already. And yes – I also wanted to be accepted. This dichotomy was all part of the sense of ambivalence felt by adoptees when making contact with the birth family, Angela explained.

For my visit, I decided on a survival strategy. How thankful I was to have rehearsed it in my mind, when the time came.

I implemented my ploy on the second day of my stay that July. I'd met Fran, divorced, and still a mutual ex-college friend of mine and Sarah's, although Sarah had kept up with her much more than I had. Fran remembered that I'd been adopted, and when I discovered that she was living in a village not far from Joyce and Arthur, we arranged to meet.

Arthur had been playing *mein host* to perfection. And Joyce was, in her detached way, trying her best to play mother. The peachy-pink, fragranced rosebud in a small crystal vase placed on the windowsill in the bedroom I occupied, cultivated in the garden just as

Rose Keller senior had cultivated the luscious blooms of Joyce's youth, was testament to this. And the way Joyce had followed me upstairs upon arrival, padding softly over the cream coloured carpet into my bedroom as I unpacked, and asking me in a quiet, pathetic voice, was I all right? Of course, I wasn't, yet I smiled sweetly and said yes. What else could I do? And she knew it wasn't all right, too. We were each, individually, doing the best we could to manage in the circumstances.

So to escape to the town, meet Fran for coffee and visit her cottage, was a godsend. When we returned, we saw a man coming out of Arthur's kitchen door, carrying a black plastic sack. I remained in Fran's Honda Civic until he was gone. He was tall, with greying speckles of dark hair at the temples. For one awful moment I thought it was Jeremy. He passed us by, glancing furtively in our direction out of the corner of his eye.

'I'm getting a sense of what you're going through,' Fran whispered.

Sarah and I, between us, had filled her in, as much as anyone on the outside could be. Necks craned, we turned and watched the man cross the road and enter the neat garden of one of the neighbouring houses. I breathed a sigh of relief.

'Not Jeremy.'

We bade our farewells and I went inside.

'I see you had someone here,' I told Arthur when he let me in through the kitchen door.

'Bart – our neighbour,' he said. 'He helps me with the garden rubbish. We've invited him, and his wife Jenny, for drinks.'

'Would you prefer it if I went out?' I offered politely, panicked. The reality of sitting in the garden drinking wine, accompanied by nibbles, with neighbours of Joyce and Arthur's, didn't appeal at all.

'Good heavens, no!' Arthur declared.

'We thought we'd say you were a friend from the North,' Joyce added, as she unwrapped a packet of cheese biscuits. She'd modified her story, and in a way it was worse. I wasn't a friend, I was her family, damn it. Her elder daughter.

I gritted my teeth.

'Just introduce me as Julie.'

Bart and his wife Jenny arrived and I was duly introduced by my first name. We sat at a round, cast iron table on the garden terrace, under a sun umbrella, overlooking a calm blue English Channel. I was pleased to be wearing my protective dark glasses. The four of them chatted happily and caught up with local gossip. Arthur poured several glasses of Chardonnay for everyone and all seemed to be going well.

The subject came up of a murder investigation in the news. Bart said they would have handled matters differently when he was at 'The Yard.' I realised then that he was a detective, and he was sitting there, right beside me.

The time arrived for them to leave. Arthur and Joyce were talking to Jenny when Bart cornered me.

'Good to have met you,' he said, extending a firm weatherbeaten hand. 'Tell me,' he added, a small, inquisitive frown knitting his brow, 'how do you know Joyce and Arthur?'

Assisted by the Chardonnay, I released my own hand, smiled and shrugged.

'Let's just say we go back a long way.'

'I see,' he replied, darkly.

I felt sure he did.

24

Happy Families

I'd arrived at Joyce and Arthur's the day before the question of my identity was raised by Bart the detective. A week before the visit took place, my travel arrangements were suddenly revised. I could have stuck to my guns, journeyed to my destination by train as planned, and, in a lot of ways I would have preferred that, even though it would have meant passing the little halt near Alice and Mike once more. Instead I felt obliged to accept transportation from an unexpected source.

'I have something to tell you,' Joyce's voice announced mysteriously, in the message I found on the answering machine when I returned to my apartment one day.

I phoned her straight back.

'Brenda says she'll pick you up from the airport.'

Brenda lived on the outskirts of south-east London, I'd discovered.

'Isn't that a bit out of her way?' I queried.

'She says it isn't a problem. She'll meet you and drive you here. I've invited her to stay the night, then she has to get back for work.'

I paused, trying to take it all in. Once, during one of

our telephone chats, Joyce had mentioned the subject of Brenda rather a lot. Small things, such as their stormy up and down relationship, how Joyce had financed both her and Daniel for many years when her grandson was growing up. Brenda's academic prowess at school, her linguistic skills, and her lack of interest in her German ancestry. Things that had given away nothing about my sister's feelings concerning me in the present.

At the end of it her voice trailed off:

'All this talk about Brenda isn't the best.'

I refrained from comment, which was tantamount to agreement.

Now she said:

'I knew she'd come round in the end.'

I inhaled deeply, wondering what had transpired between them, what else I could possibly be letting myself in for.

Brenda was a part-time carer in an old people's home, I'd learned. I was curious to meet her and yet I wasn't sure if I wanted to be spending my first night with my birth mother, and Arthur, under Arthur's roof, sharing the experience with my younger sister as well. It was enough for me to be going to stay there myself for the first time without the added complication of my unmet, formerly unknown sibling, for whom I had questionable feelings. The past wasn't her fault, I appreciated that, but I was conscious of the messed-up state she might be in, and how my appearance on the scene could have affected her. In the same way that nothing had been said about the problems with Jeremy in the initial stages, nothing had been said about Brenda's reactions to me either.

I was concerned, since I'd also received some information about Brenda from Angela, after Joyce had opened up to her regarding the past. As with other events, I've constructed the vicious scene bit by bit as its details first spilled out via Angela, then some of it directly from Joyce on a later occasion, and finally from my sister.

The episode has played itself over in my mind so many times: eighteen-year-old Brenda receiving the offer of a place at university to read French and Spanish on the condition that her birth certificate was forwarded to the authorities. Joyce and Desmond, in desperation, claiming that they were unable to find it. Why? Because the infertile Desmond, who had failed to father a child in either of his previous two marriages, had wanted Brenda to be brought up as his own. The past wiped out, all photos of Charlie Dempsey destroyed as part of the marriage settlement. No birth certificate – no university place.

It was found eventually. How I'd stared with disbelief at the copy of it, the one disclosing, with absolute certainty, that Joyce Keller had given birth to a sibling, just fifteen months after my own arrival.

The discovery that Desmond Gabbitas was not Brenda's flesh and blood resulted in a major showdown. He wasn't her father at all, not even by adoption. Strange to think I'd also once wondered if Desmond Gabbitas was my biological father too.

Then who was her father? Brenda had demanded. And what had happened to him? Was he still alive? Indeed he was, Joyce was forced to admit. In that case, Brenda would find this Charlie Dempsey if it killed her. She'd phone him up, give him a piece of her mind. Not just because he'd refused to marry Joyce as his mother had hated her, but because the moment he'd caved in was when she'd threatened to disinherit him. Who cared if Joyce was of German stock? Who cared if his mother had good reason to hate the Germans after her husband died as a result of a bombing raid? None of these excuses were good enough for Brenda.

And there was more. An elder sister, given up for adoption, slipped in by Joyce as an afterthought. Perhaps it would make Brenda feel better, that she'd escaped adoption herself, that she'd been kept when her sister was given away? Rose, her sister's name had been, Rose Keller – after her Grandma.

Brenda raced to the local library, found the telephone directory in which Charlie might still be listed. She located him at the original address Joyce had given her, the one Charlie had provided on my adoption papers. He'd married, Joyce told her, Grandma had seen the announcement in the paper. A widow with two children.

How Brenda wanted to spew out obscenity after

obscenity at Charlie. She entered a phone box, ready to do so, and dialled the number, then inserted the coins and pressed button 'A'. A man's voice answered. Instantly she hung up, unable to go through with it and mess up the lives of his family. It wasn't their fault, after all. Instead, she went into meltdown.

'That's kind of her to offer,' I told Joyce, with forced brightness.

I made a note of Brenda's e-mail address, which Joyce recited to me. It explained why I hadn't been able to trace her; instead of being Brenda Fernández she'd reverted to her maiden name of Gabbitas. Of course! Why hadn't I thought of that?

I sent a tentative message and received a surprisingly quick reply. Brenda hadn't realised I'd already booked my train ticket, and if I preferred I could still go ahead and travel that way. Maybe I didn't want her there, she suggested – she would understand if I preferred to spend time with Joyce myself. So far, so good. I respected my younger sister for her thoughtful insight, although I realised that she was testing the water for her own self preservation too. And, like me, she was probably curious. Dutifully I sent my flight arrival details and accepted her offer.

Did I regret finding *'her'*? she next fired at me through cyberspace. 'Mum... Joyce?' Yes – the ubiquitous Joyce – the one who liked to be in charge! her smouldering accusation continued. 'Always so censoring of everyone else, when she has so much to answer for herself!' I recognised the anger, backed off, said I'd quite understand if she'd had second thoughts.

Despite the warning signals I entered the domestic arrivals area at Gatwick Airport's North Terminal one August morning, heart beating wildly. A few taxi drivers held placards with names on them, and several passengers reunited with ecstatic friends or family. I waited and waited, wishing I could just take the train. And then I saw her, floating towards the group of newly arrived passengers, skinny and small, fair freckled skin wracked by sun-dried wrinkles, yet I recognised her from those old photographs.

She walked straight past me, looked up at the arrivals board. She seemed not to have noticed me even though our hair colour was similar and we were the same height. Was that really my sister? Although we shared these common features, I couldn't relate to her at all. She glanced suspiciously at me out of the corner of her eye then turned away. Perhaps I'd made a mistake and this was someone else? Perhaps she wasn't even coming? Or perhaps she'd seen me and needed to play for time? After all, I'd attached my 60th birthday photograph in my last e-mail to her – the same one I'd first sent to Joyce.

She found a seat, slumped into it and waited. I stood before her, a little way off, suitcase beside me. Still she failed to respond. Then I sauntered over to the empty seat next to her, sat down and removed my mobile from my bag. I noticed that she was clutching a set of car keys: 'Mitsubishi' it said on the tag. Joyce once told me that she'd given Brenda her old car, a Mitsubishi. Nice to have been given a car, I'd thought, a trifle jealously. As well as a house, it appeared.

I took a deep breath.

'Excuse me – are you Brenda?'

She jerked her head to the side, regarding me with evident distrust.

'Yes,' she snapped.

'I'm Julie. I was about to send you a text.'

'You don't look like your photograph,' came the challenging riposte. Dishonesty came easily to the Gabbitas family, it seemed.

A freak, violent downpour causing several major road accidents and ensuing traffic jams prolonged the car journey. The windscreen wipers of Joyce's old white Mitsubishi were trying their valiant best in storm mode, as Brenda expressed her relief that she wasn't alone in the car. Eventually we reached the clifftop house at the end of the cul-de-sac, and swung into the driveway.

I struggled further with my emotions when Joyce opened the front door. I hung back behind my younger sister, on the porch steps, and watched them exchange brief pecks on the cheek. Once Brenda was in the hallway, Joyce studied me from top to toe, gave me a similar peck and pronounced that I looked tired. I'd been up since the crack of dawn, damn it!

'Hello Julie,' came a warm welcome, once the three of us were ensconced in the off-white sitting room, with cups of coffee. I turned my head and saw Arthur standing there. Jumping to my feet I returned the greeting, then he kissed my cheek. He regarded me with kind blue eyes that reminded me of Dad's, and squeezed the tops of my arms. At this, my secret status in relation to Arthur's own family surged up with a sudden bitterness, which threatened to spoil my pleasure at being back in his company.

Despite this, the time passed by as well as it could and Joyce and Brenda seemed to be making an effort to be on their best behaviour towards each other. Underneath though, I sensed the tension, the unsaid things between them.

Later Brenda and I wandered round the seaside town, looked into boutiques and antique shops. We liked this, we concurred, didn't quite care for that: polite, superficial small talk. Several times Brenda expressed political views without waiting for a response, which, in a way, was just as well. Politics wasn't really my thing, especially when it came to discussing such matters with a stranger. All the time I felt uncomfortable. When we got back, Arthur had the camera ready. It was non-digital and I doubted it was used much.

'We need to have some photographs,' he said.

Joyce took the camera from him while Arthur stood between Brenda and I, arms around us both, as we posed together in the back garden. Joyce fiddled with the lens, I smiled, and next she clicked the shutter button while Arthur clutched my arm. Then he swapped places with Joyce, and finally I took a photo of the three of them together. Later, when the pictures were developed, I noticed that Arthur's fingers dug visibly into the folds of my blouse, gripping my arm much more tightly than Brenda's.

'I can't bear playing happy families!' my sister muttered under her breath, as we went back indoors.

I knew what she meant.

25

Skeletons in the Cupboard

I was ambivalent about Brenda, much as I was about Joyce. She probably felt the same about me. On the one hand I'd acquired that which I'd wanted so much as a child, a sibling, once replaced by Peeko. She was the closest person genetically to me on the planet, and, after years of never setting eyes on my own flesh and blood, that meant a lot. But although we'd each found a sister late in life, we'd grown up as only children in different environments. And yet there were common themes. Odious questions raised over birth certificates, life-changing events that had left their mark taking place around eighteenth birthdays. Lies, too. And abandonment. For while Brenda hadn't been put up for adoption, she'd spent her first year in a children's home, I learned.

'Heaven knows what would have happened if Mum hadn't met and married Dad,' she announced later.

But, unlike me, Brenda had, in early childhood, been reunited with her biological mother, and subsequently brought up and recognised as Joyce's daughter. And she'd known about me for the last forty years, when I'd known nothing. We were also very different. Had I met her in other circumstances, not known she was my sister, maybe we wouldn't have been drawn to each other. Or perhaps we'd have got on famously, without the burden of our flawed family background.

I sensed too that Brenda needed me, was hanging on to me, once we'd met. Daily e-mails flew back and forth, descriptions of each day's events. She even said it was good to have me as a friend, never mind a sister. It was gratifying, in a way.

Our sharing of information began on that car journey from the airport. Stuck in the stormy traffic jam we began to talk. I was forced to admit that Charlie had died, back in 1979, near where I was living, as I'd discovered on an ancestry site. Brenda reacted to this news with a mixture of curiosity, hostility and relief. She couldn't stand the thought of Charlie – it was almost as though she was glad he was dead. For all that had happened, I'd never felt that way about him, although I didn't tell Brenda that. I was sad I'd never talked to him, sensed his guilt and regret about me. I suspected we were alike, the missing link I still couldn't find in the birth family I'd encountered so far. Joyce had told Angela that he'd be in his nineties now, if I were searching for him.

'I don't think we should let Joyce know,' I said.

'No, I don't think we should,' Brenda agreed.

I was starting to learn that the less my sister had to go deeply into a subject or situation, the better, that her survival tactic was one of avoidance or circumlocution.

And there was to be another disclosure that weekend,

while I stayed on at Joyce and Arthur's after Brenda had returned home. It occurred during my last evening there, after drinks with Bart and Jenny. Arthur took us out to dinner at the same pub where we'd eaten on the two previous occasions. He was at the bar, settling the bill, when Joyce turned to me.

'I was called to my father's bedside when he was dying,' she said, throwing me a quick, uncertain glance.

Her father, not my grandfather – I noted again the distancing use of language. Joyce was handling the matter in the removed, furtive fashion I now recognised so well: intimacy wrapped in aloofness. But something profound was coming, I knew it.

'He told me of his one regret – that he'd never got to know you.'

I swallowed hard, tried to keep a brave face. I was fourteen when Robert Keller died, I'd learned that from the ancestry site. The year my mum and dad had taken me on the Rhineland cruise.

'My parents opened a letter,' she added. 'They knew about you.'

'It was in my adoption file – the bit about the letter,' I relayed as calmly as I could manage. Joyce threw me a dark look, and the subject was swiftly changed as Arthur returned from the bar.

I could hardly sleep, that last night with them, unable to stop thinking about my grandfather, whom Brenda had known. His pain; my own. Tears trickled from my eyes onto the pillow. I envied Brenda calling him Grandpa, and calling Rose Keller the first, Grandma. I'd been cheated. So had he. So had the other Rose Keller.

The day I left to go home was the worst. I'd been dreading it, the drive to the railway station, Arthur and Joyce standing before me, like a real mother and father this time. For all the complications of the visit, there was present that desire on both sides to be a family unit, cemented by my stay. One that consisted of fragments glued together. For three whole days we had indeed played happy families, the subject of the Jeremy monster and his apparently greedy spouse barely touched upon. There was no sign of him turning up and I suspected that a cast iron excuse had been produced this time round.

At one point I had caught Joyce with her head on one side, a secretive smile touching her lips, watching me one morning. We were sitting in the conservatory, sunbeams showering down upon us between the slats of the blinds pulled across the glass roof. She was, for one moment, like a contented mother, proud and happy, leaning over her baby's pram, until she looked away when she saw that I'd noticed. And I'd felt the fatherly companionship of Arthur when we sat together watching the television, discussing the programmes and news items after Joyce had gone to bed at night.

Emotion choked at my throat as we kissed each other goodbye. At theirs too, Angela told me later, after Joyce phoned her. The visit had been a tremendous success, Arthur thought of me as the daughter he'd never had, and Joyce was in awe of me and the wonderful job my parents had done. On the train I fought the tears away again, wishing that I lived closer, yet knowing it would never work.

The spectre of Jeremy hung over me, and the family get-togethers I knew took place every three months or so around that oval teak table. Jeremy and Stella, their two children and Brenda, with son Daniel, assembled for Sunday lunch at Arthur's house. Joyce in the kitchen, cooking for them all. I knew Brenda – and Daniel – were sworn to secrecy concerning my existence. Despite her efforts to claim me as a long-lost sister, I felt let down by Brenda, but I didn't say so. Not yet.

And as the train drew into the railway halt, I thought of Alice and Mike, hardly two miles away, unaware of my trip. For how long could I preserve my own secrecy? What had my parents said, or not said, in the past?

I began to wonder if I could entirely trust Brenda. An e-mail arrived one day with news I didn't like. She'd told Joyce – 'Mum' as she called her – about Charlie. How I'd found out about his death on the ancestry site, that he'd been 'down the road' from me when he'd died. Joyce had been a bit shaken at first, then rallied, asking Brenda if there was anything she wanted to know about Charlie. She told Joyce there wasn't.

I was relieved and cross at the same time. Brenda might have told me of her intention first. But I knew these things sometimes happened, in the moment, when the timing seemed right. It had to come out sometime. Even so, I was cautious. And I was disappointed that she hadn't got some information about our father from Joyce; this might have been a rare occasion, offered in a vulnerable moment, when it was temporarily available.

Next came Joyce's message, left on my landline. She was agog.

'I gather you found out about Charlie Dempsey. I want to hear more.'

I phoned her back, explained that I hadn't wished to upset her. I also said there wasn't much to add. And, unlike Brenda, I seized the moment, prised information from her about Charlie. Bright, grammar-school educated; his own father, killed by the bomb, had owned a prestigious clothing agency which had died with him. After a stint in the Royal Navy during the war (no wonder Joyce had wanted to know what ship my dad was on) Joyce's father – my grandfather – who owned a dress shop, found him a job as a textile agent. I could visualise it: Robert Keller setting up Charlie in work so that he could support and marry Joyce, give future grandchildren a secure home.

'Am I like him?' I dared to ask.

Joyce huffed and puffed.

'A little perhaps – round the eyes.' A pause. 'Charlie was nice,' she added.

I could see, across the miles, a warm glow momentarily settling on her face, putting a smile upon her lips as it had that day in the conservatory. Then it faded.

Joyce wanted me to be like her, I could tell. I was, in some ways. Perhaps the rebellious streak in me was also inherited from her, and from our shared Rhineland ancestry. Intrepid, determined, a desire to forge ahead despite all odds. Mixed with the impediment of adoption, it was a lethal cocktail.

'I'm sure Charlie was searching for you,' she was saying. 'It was just three years after the laws were changed.'

'He wouldn't have known who I'd become,' I objected. 'No-one could have found that information in those days, unless they already knew the new identity of the person they were searching for.'

My own adoption hadn't been a private arrangement, where there was often greater transparency, although it had the hallmark of one in that it had evidently been orchestrated by Aunt Astrid, behind the scenes.

'There are ways and means,' Joyce replied.

I knew there were. Private detective work. But I was more convinced we'd seen each other by accident. The faint recollection of a man in a car, parked in a side street, floated to the surface of my mind. I'd spotted him several times shortly before the date recorded for his death. Had he in some way recognised me, I now wondered? Had he come back to take a second look? I hadn't wanted to consider such matters back then, since I hadn't wanted to think about my biological father at all. But there were things that I knew, and Joyce knew, deep down, that couldn't be explained away. Like the voice we'd both heard that January morning, nearly two years ago.

Christmas was fast approaching. A whole year since Diane had contacted Joyce. Another e-mail came from Brenda. News of an impending family get-together, with Jeremy, Stella and the others. Around the oval teak table. At last I dared to challenge my sister.

'I trust you'll be drinking a toast to the absent family member,' I wrote bitterly.

'There'd be so many we wouldn't know where to start,' she joked.

The next e-mail was the last she was to send for a very long time.

'Dear Skeleton,' it began.

26

Mum's the Word

Before the silent rift set in, we basked in a honeymoon period that autumn, one in which Joyce continued to phone me weekly and Brenda kept in touch by e-mail every day. I began to speculate upon the possibility that Joyce wanted to grow closer and, once, when I called her back and Arthur answered the phone, he said:

'I'll just get your mum for you.'

The pained silence as he handed the receiver to Joyce was tangible, and I began to wonder if Joyce really did want me to call her that. Maybe she didn't like to suggest it in case I reacted badly? Undeniably, I had, at first, struggled with Arthur's use of the label, even though I'd kept my feelings to myself.

But Brenda called Joyce 'Mum' and Brenda was my younger sister. And Joyce had clearly been delighted when Brenda and I were finally in touch. Or rather, when she had put us in touch, as interpreted heatedly by Brenda, in that Joyce was the prime mover and controller to whom we must always defer in such matters.

I lay in bed at night, questioning whether or not it would work, whether or not I could call Joyce by that title after so many years apart. And what of the mum who'd brought me up as her own? I'd loved her to bits. The mum who'd lost a sister in a hospital as a child, one with the same coloured hair as mine. The mum who couldn't give birth, knowing that if it hadn't been for the bomb that targeted Dad's house he would have still been married to Rachel, his first wife, and had children with her, most likely. That same mum who'd passed away and yet she was still alive inside of me, her photo by my bedside.

And there was the added complication of secrecy. If Joyce really did want me to call her 'Mum', fit for the people who had gathered together for the 'family photographs' of that recent summer, as Joyce had described them when sending me copies in a letter, her cover would be blown. Were she and Arthur coming closer to telling Jeremy after all? It seemed that they might be; Joyce had even intimated as much to Angela. But was it wishful thinking, the playing out of a mental fantasy that couldn't ever mix with the harsh world of reality, as in the eyes of two people of that generation? And yet the desire to have me close to them both in their lives seemed to be dictating that this should be so.

And could I do it? I asked Angela, one day. From a cloud in the sky I sensed that my mum of old was giving me permission to go ahead, use the final years of Joyce's life as a time to make up for what we had never ever had. Angela endorsed my feelings, encouraged me to open up to the possibility of calling my birth mother more than just 'Joyce'.

I waited and waited; nothing more was said. Was I supposed to mention it? I didn't think so: it had to come from Joyce. And I knew my birth mother wasn't great at coming out with things directly. The shell she'd retreated into all those years ago was crusted thick, and even when she had told me small truths, delivered often in vague riddles, they were over and done with, not discussed again. But the matter of 'Mum' was ongoing.

There was also the situation with the person who certainly could call Joyce 'Mum', for she'd had no other. The person who was supposedly the biological daughter – as everyone had been made to believe – of Desmond Gabbitas. Did the matter of long preserved assumption, designed to keep Arthur's family (and others) ill-informed, threaten to darken the skies once more?

I hoped that my sister hadn't meant to hurt me with her ill-judged remark, delivered as a joke before that Christmas. One could never be sure what internally-driven motives lay beneath the surface, though. Had she simply no grasp of how I might actually feel, or was there, lurking in the psyche, certain denied jealousy? I couldn't help but wonder at this, since I was surprised, in a way, that she wouldn't understand, after all that she'd been through. She'd returned to England from Spain where she'd taught in an international school and had met her husband Xavier. Had she run away from Joyce and Desmond, only to return home after Desmond's death, with son Daniel, to live near her mother – our mother – our Mum? Brenda wasn't adopted, I reminded myself; she couldn't begin to understand, even though she probably thought she did. But she had spent the first year of her life in a children's home, while I'd been delivered to caring foster parents, who, despite everything, finally became my legal ones. It wasn't the best start in life, and I recalled her words to me, just months before: 'I envied you being adopted.'

Like me, Brenda was probably flawed. And how could she truly be expected to understand my point of view?

I felt anger at them all, playing on my emotions, the taking of the photographs of us all huddled close together; Arthur making fatherly noises which only reminded me of the exclusion, the hidden identity, as though I was viewing them through a glass divide. *'We'll engage with you on our terms, when it suits us.'* Once more, I wished I'd ended it after my first trip that spring.

The whole thing was made worse by the adoptive family. Several months previously, cousin Alice had sent an e-mail informing me that her daughter Charlotte was getting married in the spring. They were holding the wedding at the country house hotel where Sarah and I had stayed, although, of course, I didn't say so in our subsequent conversation. Things were getting a little too close to home. Yet if I was no longer in touch with Joyce, Arthur and Brenda, it didn't seem to matter so much. But the thought of going there, being nearby, but isolated from them through circumstances, hurt.

A Christmas card arrived from cousin Philip and Pamela, his wife. They hoped I'd be at the wedding; they could pick me up from the airport, take me to the church and on to the reception. I hadn't received an invitation and I sent an e-mail message telling them so. They were sure I'd been on the list of names when they'd last discussed it with Alice, and thought the invitation was still on its way.

But it never arrived. The bride and groom's guest list was too long and they'd had to drop some names off it, I later heard. I wasn't alone, and after all, I was only a cousin, I reminded myself. Still, it cut me to the quick, especially set within the context of that last year. Was I getting my comeuppance for keeping quiet about my recent visits to the area?

On Christmas Day, Joyce phoned and left a message. I didn't want to speak to her, could hardly believe that it was a year since I'd sat in the darkened living room, watching the Christmas tree's winking lights and listening to carols, imbibing the spicy aroma of seasonal candles, unable to believe my good fortune. It seemed a million miles away. Now I was angry, emptied of seasonal spirit.

I wrote instead, thanked Joyce for her phone call, and wished her and Arthur a 'Happy New Year'.

Angela called later, just as I'd hoped she would. Joyce had been on the phone to her. Was Julie okay? Her voice troubled; she was almost weeping, Angela said. I had hoped that Joyce would feel that way: she deserved to feel that way. If I'd wrecked her Christmas, I was pleased – another china doll thrown from the pram.

We returned to writing to one another for a while, then the phone calls began again, tentative at first. I must come and stay in the spring, Joyce announced. The thought of Jeremy continued to loom large, and I was still out of touch with Brenda. Having told her I needed some time to myself I'd tried at last to make contact with her, but received no reply. And I didn't want to put myself through the emotional trauma of playing 'happy families' again when I was still a secret from Arthur's son. I couldn't face him turning up one day, demanding to know my identity, why nobody had explained to him what had been going on. As he'd posted Joyce's letter to me, with my name and address on the envelope, he knew of my existence. I was sure of that, even if he knew nothing else about me.

During my three day stay the previous summer,

Arthur told Joyce that the last time Jeremy had visited, he'd revealed to his father that he'd been conducting some family history research online.

Arthur described how Jeremy had rubbed his hands together gleefully and said:

'I've just unearthed a family secret!'

'What did you tell him?' Joyce demanded from her chair on one side of the sitting room fireplace, squirming visibly.

'Nothing – of course,' Arthur replied. He reached for his whisky glass, glugged some down and smacked the receptacle onto the coffee table. 'God knows what Polly got up to before I met her,' he added, covering his face with his hands.

Sitting in silence, I might as well have not been there.

The phone call came on the forty-fourth anniversary of my dad's death. That terrible day all those years ago still relived, as real now as it had been at the time. There are some things that can never be erased. And there are words that can never be erased either.

Joyce's timing couldn't have been worse. We talked amicably for a while, until the subject of Jeremy was raised. Another family get-together around the oval teak table, another Sunday lunch prepared by Joyce; more grumbling about his family. On my part, a sense of marginalisation and rejection grew stronger.

'He's so difficult these days,' Joyce added.

It was hardly surprising, Jeremy was probably waiting to be told the truth. About his half-sister. About me. Perhaps he suspected that I was his half sister? – the thought had crossed my mind before. What a mess.

I didn't answer, and much as I wanted to change the subject, I let her ramble on. How I wished afterwards that I'd prevented her from doing so!

'That's why I think you should never call me Mum.'

Joyce's aim was spot on, a dart of deep, deep hurt piercing that seat of the soul – my solar plexus, and my heart.

My voice shook, its tone curt.

'I can assure you I had no intention of doing so.'

'But you had been thinking of it, hadn't you?' she countered, in a tone that was both accusatory and scornful, the defensiveness returned.

It had been Arthur, I retaliated. Referring to Joyce as my mother – my mum. I hadn't been sure how she'd felt about it, wanted to know if that's what she expected me to do – wanted me to do. Clearly she didn't.

The call, encrusted in bitterness, ended.

I wept.

27

If Only

Despite Arthur and Joyce's outmoded attitude, which had cast a dark, ghostly shadow, causing pain, a feral feline almost saved the day. Joyce knew I was a cat lover from looking through the leatherbound album I'd made for her; it was why she'd sent the Siamese kitten card on my sixty-first birthday. Conversely, I knew she'd been more of a dog person in the past, Arthur too.

'We have an elderly cat,' she told me, during the early days of our calls, before our first meeting. 'Her name's Ivory. She's very old – dates back to years ago at Arthur's farmhouse. One day the dogs brought her in as a kitten. She never left, but she's still very wild.'

'Do you know how old?' I asked, feeling just a little envious. My own cat, TomTom, once a beautiful sleek black creature, had recently been put down, aged seventeen. I was devastated at losing him.

'At least twenty-two,' she said. 'We don't know for sure, of course.'

If only TomTom could have lived that long, I thought.

Ivory had made several short appearances when first I visited Joyce and Arthur, both on my own, and with

Sarah. Leaving behind her secret outdoor life, Ivory entered the house through cat flaps in the outer and inner conservatory doors, making straight for the sitting room which we occupied, aiming for the kitchen, and by implication, the food bowl. She darted like a frightened rabbit, stopping suddenly in her tracks as though by the application of hydraulic braking, sensing the presence of someone new, someone who perhaps shouldn't be there at all. Her wide gold eyes held mine. I smiled, made cooing noises, until the eyes widened even more, a look of comprehension, followed by fear, entering the expression. Then she was off.

'Ivory's the first cat that's never responded to me,' I told Arthur one evening, during my halcyon summer stay with them both. We were sitting together after supper, like a family threesome, Arthur with his usual whisky, Joyce and I with a coffee each.

He shot me an apologetic smile.

'What a terrible reputation to have.'

Ivory had begun, grudgingly, to accept my presence, since she realised no doubt, as any astute feline would, that doing otherwise meant she had no access to her beloved master – and indeed to *his* mistress – who she'd also learned to accept over the years Arthur and Joyce had been together.

The cat purred and rubbed against Arthur's trouser leg.

'Hello Ivory,' I tried, extending an invitational hand towards her, although not too close, for fear of frightening her away.

'Go on,' Arthur cajoled, gently pushing Ivory towards me. I leaned forward. She sniffed my hand and let me rub her cheek, at the same time emitting loud rusty purrs. Then she retreated to the security of Arthur's leg.

Arthur tried again. The same thing happened, and again. Each time the purrs grew louder and we seemed to be making progress. I had to remember her roots in the wild, the way she was brought into her own adopted family, where she'd stayed ever since. And I was reminded of mine.

'Listen to Daddy!' Joyce called out to Ivory, from her usual armchair.

Whose 'Daddy'? I wondered. Mine or Ivory's? It was a subconscious slip, I felt sure of it, a peephole upon a time long ago when things might have been different, and which could, by a stretch of the imagination, be different now.

I was touched by Arthur's devotion to this cat, with the pale cream coat flecked with subtle gold, which had doubtless prompted her name. Ivory was really rather beautiful.

Thence began the coded correspondence that linked Joyce and I at a deeper, spiritual level, communicating things through feline lookalikes bearing short messages. Whenever our relationship threatened to falter, a card with a cat picture on the front arrived in the post. It had started with the one she'd sent me of the Siamese kitten, reminding me so much of Peeko. With TomTom's passing, a vacuum had been left, I realised.

TomTom had come to me before Mum went into the rest home; she'd loved the black, almost Burmese-looking kitten, wrapping himself, as she said, around her heart. He was, I'm sure, the reincarnation of Peeko, both having manifested tumours over the left eye in their final weeks. It really had been time to initiate my search into the past, a transition from one era to another.

And so it was with a cat card that Joyce attempted to convey her pain on my sixty-second birthday, a week after that dreadful phone call on the anniversary of my dad's death. Two months later I returned the gesture. She was eighty-nine. How long had we got? Eventually I received the birthday present she'd had waiting for me, no doubt wanting to give it to me in person, that previous spring.

I often hold it in my hand, the silver christening ring, her own, engraved with the name: *Joyce*. Yes, 'Joyce' – not 'Mum'. Joyce as a baby, not a mother at all. My tearful emotions when I first opened the box were mixed with both the gentle simplicity of the gesture and the sad implication that lay behind it.

Joyce had sent the napkin ring to the jeweller's to be polished in readiness for the visit she had invited me to make. It was the thought of Jeremy that had kept me away, as well as Arthur's continued secrecy and the shame he felt over his late wife's past, and over Joyce's. I'd declined the invitation politely, pleading an overload of teaching administration – which had not been entirely untrue.

Where communications were concerned, my search into the past created other tensions as well. With the adoptive family, as I now refer to them. They surfaced during the few days of the reunion in Remagen, at the end of 'Life: Part One', when I found myself sitting at a riverside café, opposite Klaus.

Beside us, the waters of the River Rhine lapped against piers and moored vessels. I recalled another time, on the deck of a cruise ship, in the shadow of the Lorelei; an angry teenager pursued by a frightened, overprotective mother who held open an anorak, in case her daughter caught cold in the misty chill. Although I didn't then know, it was also the river of my great-grandparents, consumed by a passion so strong that they fled the country to a new life in England. But I felt it in my soul and in my genes, manifested as goose-flesh on the surface of my skin.

'There's a black cat following you!' a tavern proprietor, who knew us, called out as we emerged from a cobbled side street. We were on our way back from a visit to the Peace Museum, where we'd become engrossed in the harrowing tale of the capture and collapse of the Remagen Bridge in 1945, portrayed by pictures and artefacts, in addition to information about the local American prisoner of war camps. It was just days before I was to learn about my roots and my German ancestry.

We turned and saw – yes – there was indeed a cat behind us. A TomTom lookalike. It meowed.

Klaus announced that he wanted a coffee, and we found a table on the Rheinpromenade. As we sat down I sensed much that had remained unsaid: fellow countrymen of his forebears captured by the allies, left to die in the Golden Mile camp on the Rhineland plain of the same name, and the futility of war. Always so cheerful, such fun, Klaus generally avoided subjects like that.

He was quiet, stirred his coffee, stared into the swirling liquid, then up at me.

'I know I'm often joking, Julie, but now I'm not. You see, I love you.'

Eva was preoccupied with other guests, cousins from South Germany with whom Klaus was already bored. None of them were in the mood for climbing the dozens of tower steps at the museum, and had opted instead to take a shopping trip to Cologne, up the river.

I knew Eva and Klaus's marriage had been a sham for years, yet each had held onto the other. And Klaus, I reminded myself, hadn't wanted Eva to search for her birth mother, didn't seem to care about the medical history of his children. Why rock the boat when there was no need? But in that moment, rendered speechless, I put my hands to my face and inhaled sharply.

'I haven't enjoyed myself so much for a long time,' Klaus added, following with his eyes a passing barge, on its way to Rotterdam.

The black cat sat on a wall, paw raised, ablutions momentarily suspended, and meowed at us again.

That evening we walked together to a side street by my hotel. We were grown up about it, Klaus and I. A trifle overweight, he stood there, regarding me with intensity. He was wheezing, I'd noticed, while we were climbing the concrete spiral tower steps at the Peace Museum.

We threw our arms round each other, his wiry grey-white beard pricking at my face.

'If only I were twenty years younger!' he sighed, covering this lamentation with an embarrassed chuckle.

If only, I echoed silently.

28

Repercussions

No way would I have entered into a romance with my cousin's husband; I wasn't a marriage wrecker, nor indeed, a family wrecker – not deliberately, at least. I think, though, that Eva knew; I saw it in the looks she threw me across the starched table linen during the several dinner and luncheon parties she presided at, that long weekend of our reunion. I'd seen them before, over the years, unknowing. Perhaps she'd realised something I'd never woken up to.

It was the circumstance of adoption that had held the two of us together, if conveniently separated by the miles. As children, we'd often been the subject of hushed telephone calls behind closed doors: Aunt Verity to Mum, Mum to Aunt Astrid, Aunt Astrid to Aunt Verity. Even though we never articulated it, we understood. We were cousins through legality rather than birth, suffering from the fallout of lies and cover ups, when deep down we each sensed that our respective backgrounds were cloaked in the veil of secrecy.

The marked difference lay in the fact that Eva's parents had entered into a platonic marriage of convenience. Mum had once surmised, in a weak moment, that Aunt Verity and Uncle Edward had decided to adopt a baby girl so that that she could look after them both in their old age. Although Eva's adoptive father, like mine, had died when she was in her teens, she seemed destined to care for her widowed mother, just old enough to be her granny.

Deliverance from this fate then came at the hands of Klaus, on a university exchange from Germany for one year. Eva, two years younger than he, was standing at the doorway of a public house, awaiting a date who'd failed to turn up and convey her to a party, on the back of his motor bike.

Aunt Verity would have thrown a fit had she seen my cousin borne away from her own front door on such an unsatisfactory mode of transport. Consequently, various covert operations were put into action. Perhaps that's why the boyfriend hadn't shown up, seeing before him shades of the future. Instead, the generous-hearted, blond-haired Klaus felt pity for this small-boned girl with the raven-black locks, and had rescued her from a future playing nursemaid, by wafting her off to Germany for keeps.

Anxious, I have to admit, to stay in touch with Klaus, I did so in a circuitous way, by forwarding the gallery of photographs that Maggie, the American Keller descendant, had kindly e-mailed to me the week after my return from Remagen. I hadn't been able to get over the geographical coincidence. I was trying, I knew, in my vulnerable state to hold on in vain to the tattered strands of a magical time by the River Rhine, when, if it hadn't been for Eva and the ramifications of her offspring and grandchildren, I could have happily thrown in my lot with Klaus. A pipe dream, clouded by reality. But for a short while, both he – and cousin Eva – shared with me their incredulity and enthusiasm for the discovery of my German ancestry. It might have, at last, freed Eva of me, and me of her, since now the unearthing of my biological roots was nothing to do with her, except that they bound us closer for a time.

In other circumstances Klaus might have offered to do some scouting around, see if there was even the slightest chance of any Keller descendants, distant cousins – biological ones – to be found. But I knew that he wouldn't, because, apart from the fact that he was married to my adoptive cousin, our visit to the Peace Museum had underlined the futile carnage of war. It wasn't somewhere he or I desired to go, although nothing was ever said.

Nevertheless, eight months later, Klaus conveyed to me the fact that Eva was upset because I'd reunited with my birth mother. It was entirely understandable and, despite all the problems I, myself, had faced, I felt guilty.

Then one day, out of the blue, Eva phoned and told me that my actions had finally spurred her on to try again. Realising that her own birth mother would be, if still alive, just a little older than mine, she wondered if it might be worth trying to connect with her once more. Perhaps, after the many years that had passed since the woman's rejection of her, she might, finally, have a change of heart.

A letter was sent to an adoption society. Eva forwarded me a copy, in which she gave details of her mother's identity and where she had last been living. Perhaps it was the writer in me, and the developed thirst for knowledge which had stood me in good stead during my own search into the past. But I couldn't help it, the habit kicked in, just as it had done time and time again, all those months before when trying to put together those missing pieces of my own background.

Thus I stumbled upon an online obituary, announcing an elderly lady's death, adored as she was by her four daughters and a string of grandchildren. There were also details of a church service held in the area where she'd lived most of her life, the place where Eva had once visited and seen the woman for herself. And a date: exactly a week after our reunion in Remagen.

Should I pretend that I hadn't found it? I pondered. Should I let Eva press on with her investigation, clutching at the tiniest of hopes that her wish might be granted?

In the end, I opted to do what I felt was right. Tell the truth. As youngsters, she and I had lain in beds next to each other on the occasions when she'd come to stay with me, or I with her. We'd shared our covert eavesdropping on phone calls, counted the number of times our adoptive mums had said 'Yes' or 'No' – monosyllabic responses to a torrent of advice given to them down the line from Aunt Astrid. How to deal with the ailing Tanner grandparents, relocated to a home after our aunt pleaded a nervous breakdown. Or how to bring up two rebellious daughters, who ought to be grateful for everything that had been done for them by way of adoption, one way and another. We knew, all right.

By that same principle I was brought to my next step in attempting to draw together the loose threads of the past once and for all. Despite the problems, and just as I had done before, I chose to not only keep in touch with Joyce – as did she with me – but to go and visit her again. Before I did so, I had to finally address the thing that I'd been putting off for ages – coming clean with cousin Alice, and through her, Philip and his wife Pamela. I couldn't go on visiting the area without seeing them. Besides, in my desire to discover any further revelations, I needed to find out if my adoptive parents had falsified the truth to others, just as Joyce and Desmond had done with Brenda.

Where adoption had tied Eva and I together, with my dad's side of the family it hadn't played any part, or so it seemed. How I'd longed to be one of them, even if just a first cousin; not singled out, not thought of as different. And I'd maintained a convenient silence with Alice after the fiasco of her daughter Charlotte's wedding, even though I knew from Philip that Alice had made her condemnation of their guest list strategy exceedingly clear around the family Christmas dinner table.

Now, with another Christmas fast approaching and a health scare darkening the horizon for Alice, I sent her an e-mail. Oblique, hinting at a life-changing event, something I'd discovered about the past which had shocked me to the core.

Alice is a bright cookie. Was this something to do with that time, long ago, when we'd shared the same bedroom, the night our respective parents had gone to the ball together at the Royal Naval Barracks? she asked. And did I recall how I'd wished I could watch them leave in their evening attire? She hadn't been able to understand why I'd thought the door might be locked, and had demanded of my Aunt Lorna the reason for this the next morning. I'd just been told that I was adopted, her mother explained. My mum was frightened that I would run away.

I confirmed that this was exactly what I'd been alluding to, and when our e-mail exchanges stepped up, I again found myself leaping to Mum's defence, admitting that I had indeed once tried to escape.

Alice seemed to understand. Not only that, she gifted me words that were to change the landscape just then. My adopted status made not a whit of difference. Indeed, it made things that much more special for her, and her family.

29

Wabi Sabi

A Japanese philosophy, based on Buddhist principles, accepts, and glorifies, imperfection. It is exemplified in pottery which is simple in style, rough and unrefined – yet there is beauty in it. The antithesis of classicism, which seeks the perfect in symmetry, a symbol of something that exists beyond the condition of humankind.

The fallen china doll, glued together by an adoptive mother in an attempt to restore relationships. The dashed hope that a child might happily fulfil burdensome expectations placed on her in order to substitute her parents' lost hopes. And the fear that a jealous aunt might one day unveil the truth about her niece's background, revealing the fact that her birth mother had lived after all.

Even the kindliness of friends when fashioning that person into the likeness of their own interpretation – the healing of a wound under the sticking plaster of adoption. Not least the generous acceptance of a relative, who, after acknowledgment of such legalised status, unwittingly tramples upon that which is made almost whole again.

It happened that next summer, when I returned to

visit Joyce. I stayed again under Arthur's roof, which still continued to protect a defective lifestyle. A domicile where, despite the veneer of politeness, tangible unspoken undertones of duplicity were ever present. The well polished teak, oval table, empty matching chairs placed round it, a sense of things that took place – if just from time to time – when I wasn't there. The stale, spent atmosphere was tempered only by the ebullient Philip eventually arriving to collect the cousin he had always known and loved.

I found myself longing for Philip to whisk me off to his homestead, where I was to stay with him and Pamela. Things had started to pall in the way one might expect after three days and nights spent with ninety-year-olds. As the years progressed, they were increasingly getting on each other's nerves. Arthur had gone downhill in the time I'd been away, become grumpy and dismissive, wracked by ongoing ill health. Ivory was also beginning to show her age, and positioned herself on Arthur's lap more often than not in preference to making forays outside.

'We'll just tell them we're busy,' Joyce had announced in her usual clumsy fashion, before my visit. Sensing the continued secrecy as to my identity, I inferred that she and Arthur were planning to put Jeremy and his family off from a trip to come and see them, due to my proposed stay. Was it still okay to come? I ventured over the phone. Of course it was – why wouldn't it be! – my birth mother's defensive answer rebounded.

My time with them had nevertheless been pleasant overall, assisted by Brenda's brief appearance. At one point she and I left the elderly couple to themselves and took a walk along the cliffs, overlooking the sparkling, sunlit cobalt waters of the English Channel. Relations between us had improved, after a surprise text landed in the inbox of my mobile phone, regretting the fact that *'things had gone wrong'*. Like Joyce, my sister had developed the art of non-specificity with considerable ease. The plastering over of thoughts and feelings.

And cousin Philip, once I was installed in the friendlier and more familiar environment of his detached neo-Georgian property, endeavoured to bind me even closer to the family fold with a trip down memory lane, into our shared past. Pictures of sailing expeditions, picnics on the seashore with Brandy, the cocker spaniel, me on a bicycle when Philip taught me to ride one unaided. He, Alice and I, sitting on the top of a seaside promenade wall, legs dangling at varying lengths above the sand and pebbles.

Older photographs too, of his parents' pre-war wedding and Dad's first marriage, to a woman who was not unlike Mum to look at. Dark hair, handsome features, vivacious. The viewing was accompanied by talk of the Portsmouth bombing raid, and the loss of a mother and of a wife who was expecting a child.

I sat there, dazed, frozen to the chair, just as I had been after Aunt May's original, shocking disclosure, soon after my dad's death, about his former marriage. While Philip enunciated the news with tragic emphasis, decrying the horror of war, the cutting off of youth and age, as well as fœtal destruction, he seemed not to comprehend, the tiniest little bit, the deeply damaging implications of his disclosure upon the vulnerable adoptive cousin.

Just like the time with Aunt May, I put on my best act, expressed shared consternation. Philip, I reminded myself, like so many others I knew, hadn't been adopted. In his heartfelt condemnation of the loss of an unborn child, the one whom my dad had now so evidently craved, he couldn't feel within his own body the bruising blow inflicted upon the residue of another fœtus, in another womb.

And so my attention turned from old ways of looking into the past. No more dark and dusty photographs, names on ancestry boards. The novelty of constructing an ever-growing family tree had already worn thin, eroded by Joyce's inability to acknowledge me for who I really was in front of others. Her elder daughter! A friend from the North perhaps, a Merriman cousin even, or just Julie. Any of these, but not the first, were on offer.

Reluctantly, I had to accept that Joyce's imperfect history where I was concerned was nobody else's business. I no longer desired to link myself with the rows of names that were, in truth, meaningless to me. Aided by Philip's revelation, I turned instead to recent research made in the areas of pre- and post-natal unrest. This explained how desperate thoughts of self-inflicted abortion lived on. It also explained the deep scars left on a child after separation from its mother at birth. And it explained the recurring manifestations of anger.

Old memories floated to the surface. My first birthday party, a cake covered in white icing decorated with sugared multi-coloured jellies. Me, sitting at the kitchen table in a high chair between my parents; the layout of the first house I lived in until the age of two, recalled. Also, an enormous spherical Edam cheese, bright red, whole and tempting. As a toddler I'd somehow managed to dislodge the item from its perch in the grocer's shop, with every intention of carrying it home, until reprimanded by Mum. No wartime rationing – still in force – for me! And I saw the alarmingly giant frog that sprang from the garden pond and sat there on the path, staring at me with huge, protruding eyes, slimy green-brown body pumping air. I recalled running indoors, screaming, and hiding myself in the upstairs toilet.

Not least of these recollections, the earliest. The start of 'Life: Part One'. My name was Rose Keller.

I lay there in my pram, crying at the top of my lungs, deserted on a warm summer's day. I didn't want to be left alone; it had happened before, you see. Temporarily, at first, in my desire to live, to grow inside the womb. I was afraid of being discarded, washed away in blood. Later, I was abandoned to strangers in a nursing home, then left behind again, this time in Baker Street, London. Now I was placed in the care of these two people who had taken me away to a great big house with an enormous tree growing beside the front drive.

I was left alone so that they, and I, could rest. My cry for help brought my dad – my foster dad – out of the house, an exasperated frown fixed upon me. I can, even now, visualise his face, leaning over my pram, perplexed, as I lay there, silent at last.

'What's the matter? he asked gently.

I understood but couldn't answer.

He went inside, closed the door. I opened up my lungs again, this time louder. He returned. Again the silence. I wanted him to know that the feeling of abandonment from being left all on your own wasn't something that happened just once. So I cried again and again, unpacified, until I got my way.

I've grown to understand this angry, crazed child. She'd surfaced again, unabated, much later on in life, banging at the walls with her fists: shrieking, weeping, shaking with rage at herself, at others. She'd surfaced before in the guise of a teenager, then young adult, emerging into middle age with just the occasional outburst. I'd learned, in the main, to quell that part. I was a teacher, a person of both discipline and flexibility, patient and positive in outlook, inspiring others through fun-loving creativity. I was considered one of the best, good at my job, good at many things.

So I, Julie Wetherby, began to forgive Rose Keller for her intrusion into my life. I came to know her at last, was able to recognise her for who she was; could finally give her a name.

Unable to obliterate them, the discolourations still remain. There is beauty, after all, in imperfection.

30

Song Without Words

After my break from past images, printed and virtual, I returned once more to the old photographs. I yearned to see them again, relive that journey, transitioning from black and white to colour as the years moved on. Tinged with nostalgia, poignant in their desire to escape the detritus of war, I began to witness before me those shattered lives, held close together in the perilous hope of finding something brighter.

The album lay in front of me, on the oak drop-leaf table. I turned the pages one by one, coming first to the family gathering arranged around a garden seat. Silent to me, their collective song contained so many words that, for the first time ever, I was able to interpret.

Aunt Astrid, the organiser of other people's lives, desperate to love and be loved. Granny Tanner, her gentle disposition masking the chasm of great loss – the death of a child – looking to a golden-haired infant as present healing. Grandpa Tanner, erect and stern, displaying to the camera lens the facade of respectability, a pretence at the extension of his own flesh and blood. Husband absent, Aunt Verity stood there too, behind the daughter chosen to accompany her forever. Beside that little girl, another, the centre of attention, a ray of hope for childless parents. My dad, eyes fixed upon me, while the shadow of embryonic loss, thrice afflicted, lay heavy on his spirit. And, finally, my mum, cradling me in warmth, love and protection, so much hoping it's forever.

More photographs: Alice, Philip, Aunt Lorna and Uncle Henry, Mum and Dad, Brandy the cocker spaniel, me with ruffled curls. At the beach, in the lea of a windbreaker, which failed to keep the sand away; I could still taste the granules in our sandwiches. A secret hummed in the breeze, lay hidden behind sealed lips, revealed elsewhere.

I fast-forwarded the pages and found the wedding photo of a bearded young man, fair and Germanic, raven-haired new wife dressed in white, smiling uncertainly beside him. Another snapshot followed – dog-eared and tatty – removed from its hinges, not yet replaced, still loose amongst the pages. A little girl, two perhaps, in faded colour, kneeling in water at the seaside, protected by a sunbonnet. What burden of hopeful expectation lay upon her tiny shoulders! The sight of her once brought tears of remorse to the birth mother's eye, the unuttered feelings of regret and self-admonition. Why hadn't she told her parents; why had she let things drift to the point of no return? It had been too late, her determination to keep another child, unsated.

* * *

This mother's wordless lament lay too, in pictures, I knew it then. Those that could see the light of day, just out of reach, and those which could never grace the walls or adorn the surfaces of shelves. She'd grasped at straws, flimsy in feel to the point of snapping. There was something of importance she had to convey in an early letter to that child – to me – when grown up, a lifetime missing. A great uncle on the Merriman side of the family was musical: an organist, pianist and singer of some accomplishment. It was the nearest she had ever dared to come in claiming any useful transference of genetic talent.

She knew it had been cultivated elsewhere in more fertile soil than she – or Charlie – might otherwise have tilled. There was no need to say that it wouldn't have been offered at all, the message lay in undertones. She would never get to hear the strains of Mendelssohn's 'Song Without Words'.

It is one of many such works, with flowing patterns and moments of restlessness and tension, followed by temporary repose. It carries the echoes of a tormented, humoured child; gives vent to troubled discovery. A possible father – others too – the gradual emergence of grim reality. Desmond Gabbitas, Charles Walton Dempsey, Commander James Wetherby, MBE, RN, and Joyce's Arthur.

It was in those moments, in the first shocking stages of my search into the past, that my fingers sought out the notes, absorbed by repetition into the muscular memory, reaching to the very depths of my anatomy, and to my soul. Discovered just fleetingly at first, they defied the name labels bestowed upon me, transmuted them into an identity that lies beyond the personality. It was, I began to realise, the place I'd occupied while engaged in teaching, writing, and music making, defined by something of much greater worth. Something that had been present before all else.

Wouldn't Joyce like to hear you play? Sarah enquired one day. A CD perhaps, of 'easy listening' numbers: 'these you have loved'. Beethoven's 'Fur Elise', a potpourri of my own compositions, even a Chopin Waltz, and yes – that Mendelssohn piece, since left untouched.

I didn't think so.

'Ask her, just the same,' my old friend still insisted.

My suggestion, inserted with careful timing into our weekly Sunday afternoon phone call, fell, not unsurprisingly, on deaf ears. They didn't have a CD player, no. Arthur listened to classical music on the radio instead, when resting in the afternoons, alone. I was thinking of making her a CD I hinted, but there was still no reaction. I changed the subject.

She cannot listen; it pains her, just as the portrait of the child in the emerald green dress cannot be viewed. These commodities are the product of other parents, other opportunities, of which she mustn't partake. Neither is she entitled to be called 'Mum'; there was another – once – more deserving, you understand. And neither does she want her past replayed, true happiness lost.

'Everyone enjoyed meeting you,' I told her, over the phone.

'Why?' she huffed.

They knew, didn't they? Judged her, were privy to her innermost secrets.

I couldn't believe that she summoned up the strength to go to the pre Christmas gathering. So successful it was – everyone happy! How she'd loved it, told Arthur afterwards what a contrast it was to 'the others'.

I was staying with Brenda, a first, attending Daniel's thirtieth birthday party. Fancy dress. A big step forward. It seemed only right that I should ask Alice, Mike, Philip and Pamela to meet us for lunch that same weekend. Brenda knew of the perfect place, thatched and timbered, beside a river, just idyllic. She would book a table, choose it even, one by a window, with a view.

'You're invited of course – but I'd understand it if you preferred not to come,' I told Joyce, beforehand.

I was going to the party, I explained, meeting Daniel's future in-laws at Brenda's behest. Perhaps, just perhaps, at a stretch, it was time to knock down some walls. Not spoken, but digested, I sensed the dawn of realisation.

'I'll come,' she declared. I detected enthusiasm.

Arthur wouldn't, although I said he'd be welcome. He'd become a misery, hardly going out at all; the only time he cheered up was when Jeremy appeared, apparently.

'Come and visit us sometime,' he'd muttered distractedly, while seeing to Ivory's food bowl when, that same weekend, it was time for me to say goodbye.

Brenda and I had come to pick up Joyce, take her to the luncheon venue. Against the doctor's advice, Arthur poured himself a whisky, then slumped into his favourite armchair, staring out of the French window. Beside him, on the carpet, his sickly wheezing off-white cat curled herself up into a skinny ball against the radiator.

I'd warned my cousins not to make reference to my relationship with Joyce. It was enough that she was going to the lunch. I explained this to Brenda while we were preparing to leave for Daniel's party, the evening before. Likewise she'd given similar warnings to him and Tanya, his fiancée, about me.

'I didn't know Brenda had a sister!' Tanya's mum had exclaimed, upon hearing of my imminent appearance. I was glad of my fancy dress disguise, largely lost on them.

'Who are you, Julie?' Tanya blurted out at the party.

It was a good question. I removed the deathly white mask with the bright red lips, a scintillating teardrop rolling down the cheek, beneath a black skull-cap. As I revealed my face, a bright smile fixed upon it, Daniel answered for me. He was a pleasant young man; he'd planted a kiss on my cheek when his mother and I arrived.

'Pierrot the Clown.'

Brenda had gone as a skeleton, her disguise not intended as a reference to me, as she was anxious to explain, later on.

'Are you two friends?' Tanya's young, glamorous, blonde grandmother asked, across a table.

'No – we're sisters!' Brenda answered. 'Julie lives in the North; we don't see each other all that often.'

I smiled in agreement, exchanging telegraphic glances with her. The explanation was just as we'd planned it.

I liked Tanya's friendly granny; she was dressed in black with lots of diamanté – disguised as what, I wasn't sure. I wanted to ask her, but attempts at a proper two-way conversation were drowned out by the monotonous beat of deafening, incomprehensible rap. Instead, she prattled away while I nodded repeatedly, said 'yes' to a number of indistinguishable comments.

'I've met your mum,' she said, over a refill of bubbly, in a momentary lull.

"No you haven't," I thought, "she's been dead for eighteen years."

Wait – no, not *that* mum – she means another. Of course! – the engagement party – Joyce had mentioned it to me some months before.

'Very down to earth lady,' Tanya's granny added.

'Yes – very,' I replied.

Postlude

Six Months Later

Seated at the piano, just one piece calls out to me – I haven't played it in a while. The flowing left-hand arpeggios pour from my fingers, impinged upon by the first note of the melody line above it. Entering with the intention to momentarily jar, established with a vengeance, it echoes the tone of my own personal pain and aggrievement. But where before these sounds have caused me to weep bitter tears, lick freshly opened wounds, now they reverberate with the dull aftermath of pent-up fury, the sort that Angela, before her recent retirement, warned me would continue to make an appearance from time to time.

My hands sail effortlessly across the keys, driven by the rhythmic sway of Mendelssohn's imagined gondola ride down a Venetian canal, and I am transported back over the months since Christmas time.

First – Joyce's call in January, telling me of Ivory's portentous demise. I knew it was the end, not only for the feral cat, but for her master. I cannot forget how she had once enabled me to access, just so briefly, a sense of family unity, of belonging, an oasis in the midst of turmoil.

Now, since Arthur's recent death, he and I can only

hold a wishful memory: a moment enjoyed between a man who, at last, found a daughter, and a woman who came upon a fatherly figure denied her for so many years.

A passage of minor turbulence is reached. Arpeggiated harmonies create suspended tension; they lie beneath an ethereal trill executed by the right hand. Things will settle soon, most surely. There are, after all, no more tears to shed, my anger spent.

Those last hours in Joyce and Arthur's company, during April, come to mind. Coffee in the cream-coloured sitting room, without Arthur's matching cat companion. There is a sense of empty loneliness, concealed in pretence, of exhausted lives shadowed by untruth.

Arthur holds fiercely to his mid-morning ritual, yet accepts some help from me. Three mugs stand on the kitchen work-surface, filled with coffee from a jar. Unsteadily, he pours milk from a saucepan into each of them.

I've seen that one mug before, know that it is Joyce's. Each time I've tried to ignore it, yet now I have no choice but to hold it in my hand.

'That's for your mother,' Arthur says, passing it to me.

I carry it through the kitchen, across the off-white hallway carpet into the sitting room, and place it before

Joyce on the coffee table. A past Mother's Day gift from Brenda.

'For a Special Mum'.

A point of musical dissonance brings me to the present. Why, oh why, has Joyce dodged phoning me about Arthur's passing?! Why has she given the message to my sister to transmit in an e-mail, artfully suggesting that she will have no time to speak to me herself? Because I am persona non grata, that's why. As ever, it is guilt that has stopped her, and shame. I cannot go to Arthur's funeral, where Ivory's casket lies beside him within the coffin. I am unable to grieve for him – for both of them – in public. And minus Arthur, things will doubtless change.

As the piano piece laps to its gentle conclusion, I am reminded of the disembodied voice that once called Joyce and I together. An incitement, I am certain of it, set up to fight out the primal earthly angst that still exists between us.

Yet we are linked – aided once by feline intervention – at a deeper, spiritual level. It is the only place we can meet in love and harmony, glimpsed but a few times, through the ether. Occasions when a phone call ends with 'God Bless', a moment when Joyce admits to me how she and Arthur, in their younger days, had sensed strong feelings for one another, each wedded to unhappiness. It is what, deep down, I have suspected.

And while the retrospective chords die away, I think of long ago, when my dad played me to sleep each night. Cole Porter, Gershwin and Rachmaninov; Debussy's 'La fille aux cheveux de lin' with 'de lin' crossed out, replaced by "d'or".

'Life: Part Three' has just begun. I claim it as my own. I am me, and I am free.

Identity Reclaimed

ECHOES OF AN ADOPTEE

Acknowledgements

My heartfelt thanks go to the following:

Nancy Newton Verrier: for permission to refer to her writings and work in the field of adoption. Also for the encouragement and enthusiastic support she has provided in the accomplishment of this book.

Website: nancyverrier.com

Mamook Graphics: for the exceptional cover and publishing logo design.

Website: www.mamook.co.uk

Dulce Ruby: that inspirational soul seeker, for generously allowing use of her quote.

Website: www.soultraveler.co

'F' and 'L' for their amazing beta reading efforts and 'D' for the punctilious approach to proofreading and copy editing.

'C' for professional support at the time of my investigation, and 'FM' for helping me uncover the underlying nature of my plight, which enabled me to highlight the theme of my story.

The host of Facebook friends who cheered me on my way during the whole process. Your 'likes' and positive comments kept me going.

JW

23805595R00136

Printed in Great Britain
by Amazon